Daily Food for
Presbyterian Folks

By Paul Arnold Peterson

A PRAYER

0 God, our Father, breathe a special blessing
upon this effort of Thy servant. Take the
poorly worded clause, the crudely expressed
sentence and make its truth sink into the
hearts of the readers. Thou canst accomplish
miracles with this work if Thou wilt.
It is committed to Thee with the sincere
prayer that Thy Kingdom may be established
more abundantly in the hearts of
those who study it carefully and prayerfully.
In Jesus' name. Amen.

RESOLUTION

Believing in the purpose of this
booklet, I resolve to carry out, the
spirit of the suggestion to the best
of my ability, God giving me
strength.

Signed _____

Dated for use in the years 2012 and 2040.

JANUARY 1

Thy word is a lamp unto my feet, and a
light unto my path. - Ps. 119:105.

The new year carries with it many uncertainties.
Many dark paths must be trod. He
who created the world and knows its pitfalls
gave us a Guide Book. Why not read it with
great care throughout the year?
PRAYER PETITION:

Open my eyes to read aright 'the light unto
my path'.

JANUARY 2

Lord, lift thou. up the light of thy countenance
upon us. -Ps. 4:6.

The leaves of a new book have just been
Opened. A new year has begun. No greater
blessing could possibly come to us than to
have the light of His countenance upon us.
PRAYER PETITION:

Grant me a sense of Thy presence with me
throughout this year.

JANUARY 3

This is my commandment, That ye love
one another, as I have loved YOU. -JOHN 15:
12.

The new year brings increased responsibilities.

Social obligations must be assumed. Love
toward those who despitefully use us is the
truest test of a Christian.
PRAYER PETITION:

Fill my heart with tolerance toward all
peoples. Teach me forbearance.

JANUARY 4

*Unto the upright there ariseth light in the
darkness.* -Ps. 112:4.

The way of the future may seem very dark
to you. Clouds may obscure the sun. The
challenge of the text is that we be upright,
then shall a light shine forth from the darkness.

PRAYER PETITION:

May I in all things seek the righteous way
that I may see Thy light.

JANUARY 5

*God is light, and in Him is no darkness at
all.* -1 JOHN.1: 5.

Yesterday's thought implied the inevitability
of dark days. If we had such faith as to
see God at all times then there could be no
darkness. "'God is Light" and we are rays
from that light.

PRAYER PETITION:

I would see God's reason for all things.

JANUARY 6

The love of God is shed abroad in our
hearts by the Holy Ghost. -ROM. 5: 5.

Love toward our fellowmen is not born
of ourselves. We love because He first
loved us. The Holy Spirit is the torch that
lights our love. Devoid of love-we are without
God.

PRAYER PETITION:

Teach us to reflect God's love by our lives.

JANUARY 7
The path of the just is as the shining light.
-PROV.4:18.

When we do the right, the way of righteousness
is made easier for others. Men are brought
to Christ by the way we walk. Let us watch
cur steps so that the path we wear shall be as
a shining light.

PRAYER PETITION:

Help us to watch the deeds we do, the path
we take.

JANUARY 8

O send out thy light, and thy truth, let
them lead me. -PS. 43:3.

4

Too often we guide ourselves through the
devious ways of life by our own reasoning.
This year let us seek His light and truth. Oh!
to be led by Light and Truth.
PRAYER PETITION:
Be Thou my Guide; let me follow.

JANUARY 9

I have loved thee with an everlasting love.
-JER. 31:3.

Human love fails in certain periods of crisis.
Death causes, for a time, a cessation of that
holy impulse. Nothing changes God's love.
We are never alone. He loves us everlastingly.
PRAYER PETITION:

Grant me a realization of that everlasting
Love.

JANUARY 10

*He that loveth not knoweth not God; for
God is love.* -1 JOHN 4:8.

The text for this morning is very specific.
The man devoid of love is without God. Love
must be expressed, not only toward those of our
family, but to all mankind. As we love one
another, to that extent do we teach God's love.

PRAYER PETITION:
May I show my knowledge of God by the
love which I express toward all people.

JANUARY 11

*For with thee is the fountain of life; in thy
light shall we see light. -PS. 36:9.*

When shall we learn that God is the fountain
of life? The second part of the text gives
us the key. "In Thy light shall we see light."
There must be something in our own hearts
first. Perhaps this applies to our Church
work. As we bring something to it, so shall
we get something from it.

PRAYER PETITION:

May I find the special way in which I can
show forth Thy light.

JANUARY 12

*Open to me the gates of righteousness; I
will go into them, and I will praise the Lord.
-PSALM 118:19.*

Many gates open to us; finance, education
culture. Each should seek to walk through the
gate of righteousness. Having entered, let us
close the gate to all the forces of unrighteousness
that seek to enter our paradise. God
opens,-we must close the gate.

PRAYER PETITION:

Open Thou the gate to me and I will praise
Thee.

JANUARY 13

Keep yourselves in the love of God. -JUDE
2I.

The gift of love is of God. To keep ourselves
in that love is our responsibility. The
sun may shine in all its beauty but we cannot
feel its warmth if we hide ourselves in a cave.
The analogy should be clear.

PRAYER PETITION:

Thou grantest Thy love unto me. Help
me to be so worthy as to retain this gift.

JANUARY 14

I will love Thee, a Lord, my strength. -PS.
I8:1.

He whose faith is strong enough need never
be conscious of weakness. God is our strength.
Strength is not merely muscle; it is spiritual.
Strength alone is brutal. Our weaknesses
touched by God give real power.

PRAYER PETITION:

"I would be strong, for there IS much to
suffer."

JANUARY 15

Remember the Sabbath Day. -EXODUS 20:8;

We live in a greatly distracted age. The
end of a day is not a period of relaxation, but
of planning for the next. The Sabbath, likewise,
has lost much of its meaning, due to our
having permitted too many secular affairs to
crowd in upon us. It should remind you of
God, church bells, fellowship with God's people,
spiritual joys for your family.

PRAYER PETITION:

May this be indeed a Hallowed Day, made
sweeter because I have worshipped Thee.

JANUARY 16

*For Thy Name's sake, lead me, and guide
me. -Ps.31:3.*

Jesus spoke of mortals as sheep. Why? Because
of all creatures we are the most foolish.
There is pathos in this analogy. Will we never
learn that we cannot lead ourselves? God
alone can lead and guide us.

PRAYER PETITION:

May I permit Thee to guide me through this
entire week.

JANUARY 17

*The Lord shall guide thee continually. -ISA.
58:11.*

Yesterday's text expressed the prayer of the
Psalmist for guidance. Today's text gives the
assurance of God's continual guidance. Life
is spiritual and if only we sought those influences,
then through all the experiences of life
we would be guided correctly.

PRAYER PETITION:

Thou hast guided. I may not have always
followed. Give me the will to be led.

JANUARY 18

*If any of you lack, wisdom, let him ask of
God, and . . . it shall be given him.* - JAMES
1:5.

The day before yesterday we recognized
strength as an attribute of God. Today we see
Him as Wisdom. Illiterate minds illumined by
God often become our greatest minds. Do not
misunderstand. A man may be intelligent
but not wise. Wisdom is common sense inspired
by God.

PRAYER PETITION:

May I be truly wise, not merely intelligent.

JANUARY 19

*Hear . . . and in Thy faithfulness answer
me.* -PS. 143:1.

The Psalmist, in the above text, offers a deeply sincere petition. The implication is that he knows God will hear and will answer. Is your faith that strong? Do you believe in the faithfulness of God? This is the challenge of the text.

PRAYER PETITION:

I would believe in God's faithfulness to me, that He will hear my prayers.

JANUARY 20

Let all those that put their trust in Thee rejoice.
-PS. 5: 11.

This text challenges us to a happier Christian experience. Something must be wrong with the man who is continually unhappy. Surely he does not trust God. Invested trust in God pays the rich dividends of joy. Let us, therefore, rejoice, for we know the secret.

PRAYER PETITION:

I would be a happy Christian, showing God and others that I trust Him.

JANUARY 21

Walk in love, as Christ also hath loved us.
-EPH.5:2.

The garden of life has many paths. We

can walk upon so many of them. The pathway
of love is bordered by beautiful flowers and
strewn with rose petals. Inhaling this fragrance,
we should give it out to others. Christ
walked the path. Oh! to follow in His steps.

PRAYER PETITION:

Christ's path of love led to sacrifice. Give
me courage to walk in love.

JANUARY 22

*In His love and in His pity, He redeemed
them.* -ISAIAH 63 :9.

There are many marvelous attributes of
God. His Love and Pity are two upon which
we might well meditate. Then, too, He has
redeemed us. Each has been, instinctively,
sold into the bondage of sin. God's love, alone,
can buy us back. Let us not only read this
text, but appropriate it unto ourselves as a
living fact.

PRAYER PETITION:

Grant me to feel a personal redemption
through the love and pity of my Savior.

JANUARY 23

*Blessed is the man that maketh the Lord his
trust.* -Ps. 40:4.

If you do not recall the Beatitudes as they
are found in Matthew five, read them this
morning. The above text summarizes all of
the Beatitudes. To be blessed is to have God's
favor. Carry the secret of that favor with
you throughout the day.

PRAYER PETITION:

I would more sincerely trust in Thee.

JANUARY 24

*I love the Lord because He hath heard my
voice.* -Ps. 116: 1.

The Psalms are a groping after God. His
attributes are practically all found in the book
by the Psalmist. God hears us. His divine ear
is so sensitively attuned as to hear the slightest
murmur of our hearts directed toward Him.

PRAYER PETITION:

May I believe more firmly that God is hearing
my prayers.

JANUARY 25

*... If My people pray, I ... will forgive
their sin.* -2 CHRON. 7:14.

There is nothing a parent desires more than
to have his child come to him, admit his fault
and ask to be forgiven. The parent really has

forgiven the child before he asks. God is our divine Father. He likes to hear us pray to Him. He then forgives our sin.

PRAYER SUGGESTION:

May we as a church, lift our voices unitedly in prayer to God, seeking forgiveness for the sins which we have committed.

JANUARY 26

Blessed is he whose transgression is forgiven. -PS. 32:1.

There is no load like the weight of sin. If there were no God to whom we could go to find relief, the death rate of people with sensitive consciences would be very high. In forgiving us, God lifts the weight of our load.
You have God's favor when he forgives your sin.

PRAYER PETITION:

Forgive Thou me my transgressions.

JANUARY 27

Whatsoever, ye shall ask in prayer, believing, ye shall receive. -MATT. 21 :22.

Here is the psychology of prayer. You alone can make the test. Pray, *BELIEVING,* and you shall receive an answer. There is no

unanswered prayer. The answer may be different
from what you expected, but an answer
always comes if you believe.

PRAYER SUGGESTION:

Take to God today in prayer your most anxious
concern and BELIEVE.

JANUARY 28

Unto you therefore which believe, He is
precious. -PETER 2 :7.

I know men who are criticized very highly
in their respective communities. I have been
in the homes of these men and have seen them
with those who love and believe in them. To
these, the men are precious. When we believe
in God, He is precious.

PRAYER PETITION:

Help us to refrain from criticism, knowing
that to someone he whom we would criticize is
indeed precious.

JANUARY 29

Behold, God is my salvation; I will trust,
and not be afraid. -ISA. 12 :2.

To be saved is to be delivered from the pollution
of sin. God alone can do this. The
text is a challenge to faith. Salvation is a process.

14

Removal from all the influences of sin
is not instantaneous. In spite of this, we
should trust and not be afraid.

PRAYER PETITION:

Help me to be fearless, secure in my Savior.

JANUARY 30

Ye have not, because ye ask not. -JAMES
4:2.

It would be well to read the first few verses
of this chapter from the Bible. The first part
of this text describes one who lusts and yet has
not; desires 'to have and cannot obtain'. The
reason for his instability is that he never
asked of God. Our lives are properly rounded
out only when we ask of God.

PRAYER SUGGESTION:

Pray for that which you have desired but
have never before asked.

JANUARY 31

*And it shall come to pass, that before they
call, I will answer.* -ISA. 65 :24.

Many of our texts this month have suggested
the thought of prayer. It is well that we
close with another. Take inventory of your
life this past month. Are you satisfied with

what you have done? What sort of religious
rating do you conscientiously feel that you can
give yourself? What grade will God give
you?

PRAYER PETITION:

I thank Thee for this month spent with
Thee. May its mistakes teach me new lessons
for the new month.

FEBRUARY 1

I have learned, in whatsoever state I am,
therewith to be content. -PHIL. 4: 11.

There is no happier philosophy than the
above. Envy kills as quickly as disease. The
text does not suggest indolence, rather, the contenting
of ourselves with only the result of our
very best effort. The application is to all of
life's physical conditions.

PRAYER PETITION:

Grant that I may learn to be truly content
knowing that God's will is being done in my
life.

FEBRUARY 2
Thou shalt guide me with thy counsel, and
afterward receive me to glory. -Ps. 73 :24.

God is not merely a Great Judge who hears
our case and renders a verdict. He counsels

and advises with us. We can constantly hold telephonic conversation with heaven. The promise of the text is that He will guide us on earth and to heaven.

PRAYER PETITION:

Help me to hear Thy counsel, and hearing, may I heed it.

FEBRUARY 3

Give us this day our daily bread. -MATT. 6:11.

I venture that each one who reads the above text this morning, can, if he chooses, eat three meals today. The humblest in our congregation has sufficient for his table. We usually thank Uncle Sam for the opportunities of our land. Suppose God withheld the rains for seven years! What if a plague exterminated the cattle. Well might we pray "Give us this day our daily bread."

PRAYER SUGGESTION:

Pray the Lord's Prayer.

FEBRUARY 4

I know, O Lord, that thy judgments are right. -Ps. 119:75.

It is said that our conscience is never wrong,

but that our judgment of what conscience dictates
is often mistaken. God's judgment of
the needs of His people is always right. To
"know" that this is true needs the affirmation
of a sincere faith.

PRAYER SUGGESTION:

Ask God very directly to give you proper
judgment on any problem which you may be
facing.

FEBRUARY 5

*Come and hear, all ye that fear God, and I
will declare what he hath done for my soul.*
- PS.66:16.

It would be well this morning to give personal
testimony of what He has done for
your soul. Does God mean anything to you?
Is your religion merely a habit or an intellectual
assent? Look deeply into your soul and tell
God frankly what lies there.

PRAYER SUGGESTION:

Go to God in gratitude for what he has done
for you.

FEBRUARY 6

*He led them forth by the right way, that
they might go to a city of habitation.* *-Ps.107:7.*

It is confusing for a tourist to ask directions of several people. Usually each differs on the way to go. Life has many roads to the "city of habitation." Education, philosophy, individual opinion, each seeks to guide us. The only safe route is not the broadest, but the narrowest highway. It is the way of God.

PRAYER PETITION:

Show me the right way to go, Father, that I may enter the final City of Habitation.

FEBRUARY 7

I pray not that thou shouldest take them out of the world, but that thou shouldest keep them from the evil. -JOHN 17:15.

The above is a portion of Jesus' Prayer for all believers. Some prefer to be removed from the evils and sins of this world. Many look to that heavenly experience where we shall be removed from the entanglements of the flesh. Jesus would not have it so. He would that we be delivered from evil here. The secret of this suggestion is to flee from it whenever it comes into your life.

PRAYER SUGGESTION:

Pray that you may be delivered from your most prevailing temptation.

FEBRUARY 8

*But he that glorieth, let him glory in the
Lord.* -2 COR. 10:17.

To glory is to boast about or take pride in
something which we feel we have accomplished.
It is innate to glory. Invariably it is
directed toward oneself. Nothing is more
dangerous than self glory; nothing tends to
benefit one so much as to glory in the Lord.

PRAYER PETITION:

May there be no thought in my life of glory
for myself, but may I do all to the glory of my
creator.

FEBRUARY 9

Let your loins be girded about, and your
lights burning; and ye yourselves like unto men
that wait for their Lord. -LUKE 12:35, 36.

To properly understand the text for this
morning, you should begin reading from the
thirty-first verse. The passage reminds one
of the parable of the Ten Virgins. We are
reminded of the uncertainty of material comforts
and advised to prepare for eternity. Our
lives should be constantly expectant of the
Lord's coming.

PRAYER PETITION:

Fit me, O God, for entering into the presence
of my Lord.

FEBRUARY 10

Thy word have I hid in mine heart, that might not sin against thee. -Ps. 119: 11.

The greatest good you can do your children, if you have any, is to teach them these simple texts of scripture. Have the texts repeated through the day. Someday they will rise up and bless you for this contribution to their lives. With scripture texts in our hearts, we cannot sin against God.

PRAYER SUGGESTION:

Offer unto God a text of scripture which may especially fit the needs of your life.

FEBRUARY 11

Hold thou me up, and I shall be safe -PS. 119:117.

This text reminds one of Psalm 91:12, which reads, "They shall bear thee up in their hands, lest thou dash thy foot against a stone." The latter text suggests that angels shall bear us up. The thought for this morning is similar. If God holds us up, we shall be safe.

PRAYER PETITION

In all times of danger, whether physical or spiritual, help me to turn to Thee, knowing that there is safety.

February 12

Watch ye, stand fast in the faith, quit you
like men, be strong. -1 COR. 16:13.

Here we have a sermon which outlines itself
into four points. Each point is well defined in
the text. The second thought is most significant
"stand fast in the faith." Many things
tend to rob us of our old fashioned faith. Definitions
may change, but principles never do.
Let us not be ashamed of a living, vital faith.
It, alone, can save.
PRAYER PETITION:

Give me faith-faith in myself, faith in
mankind, faith in God.

FEBRUARY 13

In the world ye shall have tribulations but
be of good cheer; I have overcome the world.
-JOHN 16:33.

Here we have the promise of inevitable tribulation
Instead of bitterness, cheer should
be our weapon. As He has overcome, so can
we through the power of His might.
PRAYER PETITION:
Give unto me greater joy. May I trust
Thee to overcome for me my greatest tribulation.

FEBRUARY 14
Heaviness in the heart of man maketh it
stoop: but a good word maketh it glad. -PROV. 12 :25.

Activity overcomes many evil tendencies.
Growing children should be given more of it.
Lazy religious souls should be lashed into
activity by the whip of service. A task bigger
than ourselves is "a good work." No job
is bigger than the Christian life. Living it
well makes one glad.

PRAYER PETITION:

Bless me in my work. Help me to be happy
in it, no matter how irksome it may seem.

FEBRUARY 15

*Let all bitterness, and wrath, and anger, and
clamor, and evil speaking, be put away from
you with all malice.* -EPH. 4:31.

The disturbances mentioned above come
from our own individual selves. Often we
blame external influences. Only a discordant
soul is affected by outward disorders. What a
happy experience would be ours if bitterness,
wrath, anger, criticism were put out of our
lives. A life devoid of these things would be
Christian. Let us try to lay them aside this
whole day.

PRAYER SUGGESTION:

Pray that we as individuals and a congregation
may be free from all bitterness, all wrath,
all anger, all clamor, all evil-speaking, all malice.

FEBRUARY 16

Evening, and morning, and at noon, will I
pray, and cry aloud; and He shall hear my
voice. Cast thy burden upon the Lord, and He
shall sustain thee: He shall never suffer the
righteous to be moved. -PS. 55: 17, 22.

The Mohammedan prays several times daily.
If the heathen can pray to one of 300,000,000
gods, impersonally related to them, how much
more should we, to a personal Father. If we
pray, He promises to hear. Thy burdens He
shall carry. He shall sustain. A righteous
life He will reward. Today let us pray, morning,
noon and night.

PRAYER SUGGESTION:

Take your heaviest burden before the Lord.
Come away feeling that He will remove it.

FEBRUARY 17

By faith Abraham, when he was called to go
out into a place which he should after receive
for an inheritance, obeyed: and he went out,
not knowing whither he went. -HEB. 11: 8.

Faith sees intangibles. Intellect cannot fully
analyze all things. Faith implies a God. If
we had faith in Him, then we would obey
Him. "An inheritance" would reward us.
Though we are led into strange places, and we
know not which way to turn, He will guide

24

us, if only our faith is strong enough.

PRAYER PETITION:

I may not know the reason, but help me
that I may hear Thy will for me and obey.

FEBRUARY 18

*For he looked for a city which hath foundations,
whose builder and maker is God.* -HEB. 11:10.

Our text for this morning might well be
converted into a very practical thought. Cities
come and cities go. We measure their influence
by the number of people, width of streets and
height of buildings. God looks at the heart
of a town as He looks at the motive of a man.
Let us undergird our city with "foundations."
God should be the supreme Architect.

PRAYER SUGGESTION:

Pray for our city that we may be well pleasing
in the sight of our Builder and Maker.
Pray for our city officials.

FEBRUARY 19

*I am the Lord thy God which teacheth thee
to profit, which leadeth thee.* -ISA. 48:17.

Material investments are made through our
own reasoning. Did you ever conceive God to
be a Silent Partner in your business? The text

suggests He will teach you to profit. He counsels us, "then had thy peace been as a river, and thy righteousness as the waves of the sea." Make an investment today, if you can, with God "teaching thee to profit."

PRAYER SUGGESTION:

Show your gratitude to God for any personal profit that may have come to you.
Thank Him for having prospered our church.

FEBRUARY 20

But they that wait upon the Lord shall re-new their strength; they shall mount up with wings as eagles; they shall run, and not be weary; and they shall walk, and not faint.
-ISA. 40:31.

There should be an ecstatic element in religion. It comes from waiting upon the Lord. When He is our Strength, we shall not be weary. If tribulations come, we can 'mount up with wings as eagles'. Leave the garments of criticism and worry in the hands of the enemy. The above comes to our lives. not through unceasing activity, rather by waiting upon Him.

PRAYER PETITION:

I can do all things if Thou, Oh Christ, dost strengthen me.

26

FEBRUARY 21

My grace is sufficient for thee. -2 COR. 12:9.

It would be well this morning to read the
I receding verses of this chapter. Paul tells
of having prayed thrice to be relieved of Hi
I horn in the flesh." The answer came in the
words of the above text. Temptations may
crowd your life today. God's grace is sufficient,
Perhaps ambition is drying your soul.
God's favor, after all, is the only thing that
matters, Relax upon the promise of this text.

PRAYER PETITION:

Help me to know Thy grace even as it is
granted unto me.

FEBRUARY 22

Forgive, and ye shall be forgiven. -LUKE 6:37.
No one suffered at the hands of man
as did Jesus. Almost His last words were,
"Father, forgive them." To a genuinely real
Christian there is no indignation. Doubtless
folks have been unjustly unkind; you have no
case, you must forgive. God forgives His
children only as they forgive their fellowmen.

PRAYER SUGGESTION:

Pray for someone whom it is difficult to
forgive.

FEBRUARY 23

Hitherto hath the Lord helped us. -1 SAM. 7:12.

In every man's life a stone could be erected
between Mizpeh and Shen, inscribing thereon
"Hitherto hath the Lord helped us." Isn't it
peculiar that though He has always helped us
in the past, we distrust His ability to do so in
the future? At every cross-road of the future
this stone should be erected.

PRAYER SUGGESTION:

Be grateful for some one thing in which the
Lord hath helped you.

FEBRUARY 24

I will, therefore, that men pray everywhere.
-1 Tim. 2:8.

Prayer is not merely a closet experience. It
can't be punched on the time clock of our
religious natures as another religious duty performed.
It is a constant attitude of thought.
It is the fragrance of a soul ever turned toward
God. Prayer is the slightest ripple on the sea
of our moral consciousness directed toward
the good. Prayer is sincere, unaffected,
conversation with God.

PRAYER SUGGESTION:

Pray that all men may be taught to under-

Lind the efficacy of prayer.

FEBRUARY 25

Pray now unto the Lord our God. -JER. 37:3.

Pray as the day begins.
Pray when the problems come.
Pray for your church so dear.
Pray for the friends you know.
Pray for a spirit sweet.
Pray for your hateful foes.
Pray unto the Lord your God-
NOW

PRAYER SUGGESTION:

Offer a personal direct prayer unto the
Lord, taking to Him anything that is on your
heart.

FEBRUARY 26

*And by the river upon the bank. thereof, on
this side and on that side, shall grow all trees
for meat, whose leaf shall not fade, neither
shall the fruit thereof be consumed.* -EZEK.
47:12.

I am preaching at Sarnia, Ontario, today.
The invitation to do so was extended me five
months ago. Though I have simply crossed
the river, I am in another country. Heaven
means just that to me,-crossing the river and
living somewhere else. The preaching I do to-

day will not be better; it will be based on what I did on the other side. Perhaps the heavenly life is like that, beginning *there* where we left off *here*.

PRAYER SUGGESTION:

Pray that God will use me to bring a rich blessing to the hundreds assembled at the Annual Union Services at Sarnia today.

FEBRUARY 27

If a man love Me, he will keep My words.
-JOHN 14:23.

The test of love is our devotion to the one we love. True love expresses itself not only when in the presence of the object of our affection but in our every day walks. Loving God reflects itself in every day living. Our smiles. conversation and social relations speak the word of our love for Him.

PRAYER PETITION:

Teach me how to prove my love for Thee, Father. May I hear and keep Thy words.

FEBRUARY 28

With my spirit within me will I seek Thee early. -ISA. 26:9.

The prophet Isaiah, in this text, suggests

30

that "with my soul have I desired thee in the night;" then in the next portion, "I seek Thee early". There is no time like the early morn-mg hour to come to God. Our minds are fresher and the seed of truth planted then can bear its fruit through the day.

PRAYER SUGGESTION:

Go to God in prayer early, before you have entered into any of the perplexities that try the spirit.

FEBRUARY 29

Cleanse Thou me from secret faults. -Ps. 19: 12.

Nature's carpet of velvety green covers many ugly scars upon her bosom. Underneath are worms and the abiding places of treacherous creatures. So a gracious countenance often hides the blackness of a sinful heart. You, alone, know your secret fault. Confess it to God this morning.

PRAYER SUGGESTION:

Be frank with God. He knows everything. If you want to be cleansed, He will cleanse.

MARCH 1

Am I my brother's keeper? -GEN. 4:9.

This is the month of preparation for a new
Church Year. Ours, as you know, begins
April 1st and closes March 31st. A budget
must be accepted and raised. Too often the
worry and anxiety of finances blight our
spiritual vision for the Church. The money we
give to the Church is used to develop brotherhood among all men. Only a lack of personal
responsibility in this endeavor makes one ask,
"Am I my brother's keeper?" Only a Cain
asks such a question.

PRAYER PETITION:

I would include mankind in my thoughts
and in my prayers.

MARCH 2

*If any man will come after me, let him
deny himself, and take up his cross daily, and
follow me.* -LUKE 9:23.

Three things are involved in becoming like
Christ; self denial, His cross, and following
Him. We have heard many sermons on this
text. It has been suggested that only the
meek and pure souls can see God. Just so, in
following Christ, these three things are
imperative.

PRAYER PETITION:
Teach me sacrifice. May I accept my cross
and carry it on as Thou didst.
the Father is this, To visit the fatherless and

MARCH 3

*Pure religion and undefiled before God and
widows in their affliction, and to keep himself
unspotted from the world.* -JAMES 1:27.

Our thought of yesterday had homiletic
value in that it had three points. The text
this morning also has three suggestive thoughts.
We have a statement as to the meaning of
"True Religion."
I. It Is Personal. It recognizes God as a
Father.
II. It Involves Service. "To visit the father-
less and widows in their affliction."
III. It Suggests Character. "To keep himself
unspotted from the world."

PRAYER PETITION:

May I cease to be self-centered. May I reach
out in service to others, so developing my
character.

MARCH 4

*Thy kingdom come. Thy will be done in
earth as it is in heaven.* -MATT. 6:10.

"Thy kingdom come." This petition is in the
prayer of our Lord. It is said by most of us
often. If we meant it when we prayed, then
we would do more than merely pray. We
would labor toward the end of establishing our
prayer. The kingdom referred to is the one in

heaven above. 0 to have that kingdom here on
earth. Hate, then, would melt away. Discords
would swell into eternal harmonies.
Life would be heavenly. Let us pray and
labor toward the end of establishing His
Kingdom.

PRAYER PETITION:

Help me to do my part in establishing Thy
Kingdom. I can aid by seeking Thy will in
all things.

MARCH 5

That which I see not, teach thou me. -JOB
34:32.

Death may have plucked from your garden
a precious loved one. Illness may have taken
from you the rigor of health. Financial re-
verses may have caused you many material
privations. Love may have knocked at your
door and before you could open, passed on
elsewhere. To see and understand we cannot.
God alone can teach us the reason for it all.
There is a divine purpose.

PRAYER PETITION:

Teach me to understand that which I
cannot see or reason.

MARCH 6
I was not disobedient unto the heavenly vision.

-ACTS. 26: 19.

There is no greater unhappiness than to
have taken spiritual values lightly. Many a
man has turned his back upon heavenly things
and sought happiness elsewhere, only to find
that the blazing coals were merely embers. A
Paul becomes a power only when in tune with
heaven. There is no unhappiness except when
one is disobedient toward God. Likewise
happiness can be found only in spiritual things.

PRAYER PETITION:

Bring to my remembrance a vision of things
divine. May I no more lose sight of my
heavenly vision.

MARCH 7

*I am purposed that my mouth shall not
transgress.* -PS. 17:3.

It might be well to read James the third
chapter in connection with this text. I know
many good souls whose influence is ruined
because their mouths always transgress. Often
the lovliest characters mar their beauty because of this sin. If this is your sin, why not
reach the resolution of the Psalmist, "I am
purposed that my mouth shall not transgress."

PRAYER PETITION:

Teach me to govern the words which pass

my lips .

MARCH 8

LUKE 22:1-16.

Beginning this morning and continuing
through Easter, we shall make a study of the
events preceding our Lord's Crucifixion, and
following His Resurrection. Entered into
conscientiously, nothing could prepare our
hearts more sensitively for the Easter season
than such a study. I shall merely suggest the
passage of Scripture to read, trusting your
own heart and mind to guide you in this study.

PRAYER SUGGESTION:

Pray that there may come a" very real
Resurrection of our Savior into your heart" and
into the hearts of each of us during this Easter
season.

MARCH 9

LUKE 22:7-14.

God uses human means to accomplish His
Providence. A man with a pitcher of water
was used by Jesus to lead the way to the Up-
per Room. Often the ordinary and common
things of life, blessed by God, reveal the most
priceless things. We find the providential
note in life only when we do His bidding as
did Peter and John.

PRAYER PETITION:

Help us to appreciate the sanctity of the
little task. May we by some small thing help
prepare for the coming of our Master.

MARCH 10

JOHN 3: 1-20.

This passage requires careful and prayerful
analysis. Jesus not only preached but He
demonstrated facts. Where can we find such
a marvelous illustration of true humility?
Study again the 13th and 14th verses. Jesus
did not seek to be a great influential teacher,
but rather the servant of His disciples. He who
would be great, take heed! Success comes
only as we serve others, in deepest humility.

PRAYER PETITION:

Cleanse Thou me from pride. Make me
understand true humility,

MARCH 11

JOHN 13:1-20.

I trust you will read with great care the
chapter assigned for this morning. It is the
Sabbath and the day assigned by our denomination
for the Every Member Canvass. The
second verse carries to our hearts a practical
thought, "the devil having now put into the

heart of Judas ... to betray Him." Things may have occurred this past year which may have displeased you. You seek revenge by lessening or withholding your gift to the Church. Remember! the devil has put this thought in your mind and the only one you betray is Jesus.

PRAYER SUGGESTION:

Pray that you may have wisdom in deciding upon your gift to your Lord and His Church; that your gift be given not to men, but to God.

MARCH 12

JOHN 13:21-35.

I can imagine no greater suffering through which Jesus had to pass than the betrayal of Judas. Here was a group of twelve seemingly honest men who had received His deepest confidences. They, alone, had seen His heart. It is no small wonder that Jesus should have sought to reunite His disciples upon Judas' departure, by challenging them to love one another. As we love one another, so shall men know that we are His disciples.

PRAYER SUGGESTION:

Pray that you may in no word or deed betray your Lord. Pray that we may show forth that we are His disciples because we love one another.

MARCH 13

MATT. 26:26-35.

It is marvelous how human the Bible is. In
our study this morning we are given the words,
"Our Lord's Supper." Thrilled beyond words,
were these Galilean fisherman. Devotion was
expressed in their countenances. Jesus
suggested that they would be offended in Him.
Peter vowed to the contrary. Thrilled by the
Sacrament, inspired by the Master,-yet before
the cock had crowed three times the Master
had been betrayed. How human!

PRAYER PETITION:

May we never express more devotion to
Thee than we are' willing to live. May we
rather constantly show our devotion by our
lives.

MARCH 14

JOHN 14:1-14.

This is a much read passage. The first seven
verses should be memorized. There are three
outstanding thoughts. The first has to do
with the heavenly mansions. Jesus reiterates
that, "if it were not so I would have told you."
The second suggests the marvelous thought
of the incarnation; "he that hath seen me hath

seen the Father." How can one fully conceive
God except through Christ? Finally, the promise
that, "if ye shall ask anything in my name,
that will I do." Three marvelous assurances-
Heaven, Christ and Answered Prayer.

PRAYER PETITION:

We thank Thee that we have the assurance
that in those heavenly mansions we shall know
Thee, Christ and God.

MARCH 15

JOHN 14:15-31.

We are more or less unmindful of the Holy
Spirit. He is the Comforter promised us.
Through the Spirit all things can be accomplished.
Nothing comforts me more than this
thought. A sermon, stammeringly preached,
can be used by the Holy Spirit. Ones best,
rendered in sincerity, humble though that
may be, can be made a master-piece by the
Spirit.

PRAYER PETITION:

We thank Thee for the manifestation of
Thyself through Thy ever-presenting Spirit.

MARCH 16

JOHN 15: 1-11.

The Christian life is a dependent one. We live not in -our strength but in His. We are branches of the True Vine. As we neglect to draw strength from the Vine, so do we weaken and drop off. One never backslides- he simply has failed to abide in Christ. As a part of the Vine, we must bear fruit. Pray, what is the quality of the fruit you bear?

PRAYER SUGGESTION:

Make me to bear forth good fruit and In abundance.

MARCH 17

JOHN 15:12-26.

The New Testament is filled with passages on love. In fact, so important is this element, that some writers hold that one cannot be of God except he love his fellowmen. In our study this morning, Christ commands that we love one another. We are friends of Jesus if we do as He commands. In the eighteenth verse, the implication is that even if men hate us we must love them. You can estimate your religion by the character of your love.

PRAYER SUGGESTION:

Pray that you may love those whom it is difficult to love. Pray that you may be worthy of Christ's great sacrificial love.

MARCH 18

JOHN 16:16-31.

It is difficult in two or three sentences to
write anything of much significance, especially
on a chapter so important as this one. The
 promise of the brevity of pain and sorrow is a
comforting one. Though He made the promise
to his disciples, it applies to us as well.
Then, too, Jesus herein, forebodes His unhappy
death, but promises to return. Who knows?
He may at this moment be seeking to return
into your heart and home.

PRAYER PETITION:

Put into our hearts the joy that no man can
take from us, we pray. Such a joy can come
only from seeing Thee within our lives.

MARCH 19

JOHN 17:1-26.

Here we have the farewell prayer of Jesus.
How His heart beats with love for His fellowmen. In the twenty-first verse He prays,
"that they all may be one." Jesus knew the
discordancies of humankind. He desired that
followers of His be one in thought, heart and
purpose. You, who seek to injure another,
catch the spirit of this prayer. Live in it
 today.

PRAYER SUGGESTION:

Read this prayer carefully. Then, if you
can do so honestly, pray, as did Jesus, "I have
glorified Thee on the earth; I have manifested
Thy name unto men."

MARCH 20

MARK14:32-42

To me the tragedy of Gethsemane is not that
Jesus realized that the end was near and thus
sorrowed bitterly; rather, it is the human
weakness of His disciples. How the Master's
heart must have been bruised when he realized
that their interest in Him, seemingly, was not
greater than their material comfort. They slept
while the Master agonized. Perhaps it is
true today, that we seek our own comfort
rather than devotion to the master

PRAYER PETITION:

Forbid, Lord, that I shall sleep when Thou
givest me a task.

MARCH 21

MARK 14:43-52

Had Judas stood behind a tree, unseen by
Jesus, and pointed Him out to the soldiers, the
hurt may not have been so keen. But to have
had him kiss the Master, even though it were

simply a custom of greeting, must have broken
the Master's heart. Some still betray Him
by compromising with sin-making a profession
which does not ring true in daily
life. Unhappily, there are many Judas' alive
today.

PRAYER SUGGESTION:

If you know that in some way you are betraying
your Friend, even while pretending
great love for Him, cannot you make your
confession and be free from the torment of
your unfaithfulness?

MARCH 22

JOHN 18:12-24

You recall that Jesus predicted Peter would
Deny Him before the cock had crowed thrice.
Jesus under trial,-Peter "standing at the door
Without;-a maiden inquiring if he knew
Jesus,-Peter replying "I do not";-Peter
Warming himself at the fir. Have you
Done this? Were you over ashamed of being a
Christian? I fear that too many of us warm
Ourselves before fires, while our Master stands
Apart, on trial and condemned.

PRAYER PETITION:

We deny Thee so constantly, O Christ, while
We accept the warmth and comfort of personal
Gain. Forgive, we pray.

MARCH 23

MATT. 26:57-68

Legally, Jesus was never guilty of the accusations made against Him. World prominent attorneys have found that there was no case Against Him. Though Jesus could have risen in a masterly manner to His own defense, he "held His peace." Arguing in our own behalf does little good. If men hate us, they will do so in spite of our proving we are right and they are wrong. The greatest good is usually accomplished by holding our peace. Dean Coulter of Purdue University once expressed it in this way: "Administer large gobs of silence."

PRAYER PETITION:

Grant us to hold our peace even in the midst of unfair criticism.

MARCH 24

MATT. 26:69-75.

This narrative regarding Peter is akin to one we studied two days ago. Matthew states that Peter cursed and swore, "I know not the man." Every man knows when he does wrong and usually regrets it afterwards. Peter "went out and wept bitterly." If only we could reflect before each act, then our regrets would not be so many.

PRAYER PETITION:

May I cease to deny my Lord, before the
day of bitter regret is upon me.

MARCH 25

MATT. 27:1-10.

Our lesson this morning teaches that "the
wages of sin is death." No man ever accomplished
anything by building a deed upon a
wrong foundation. This law is a part of the
universe. Life is eternal. A wrong finds no
place in the Eternal Purpose. A Judas never
can find good use for money earned illegitimately.
You who feel that you will never be
found out in your corrupt practices are making
yourself greater than God. Your sin always
finds you out.

PRAYER SUGGESTION:

We each sin. Let us pray sincerely and
honestly that we may not arrive at the 'potter's
field' as the final reward of our sinful betrayal.

MARCH 26

JOHN 18:28-38.

Jesus was a victim of political fear. Pilate
found no fault in Him, but he did fear the
power of Caesar and therefore refused to take
initiative in releasing the Master. 0 that

each of us were free to act without thought
of what this or that group might think.
Unfortunately Church work is sometimes
hampered by the unscrupulous influence of some,
who, Caesar like, bend men's wills to their own.
This is likewise true in business and politics.
Christ can be crucified, but Caesar must not
be offended.

PRAYER PETITION:

May I never be so moved by public opinion
that I shall stand by whilst Thou, 0 Christ,
are maligned.

MARCH 27

LUKE 23:4-16.

Herod was interested in Jesus only out of
morbid curiosity. He had heard that miracles
had been performed by the Master. Only the
sensational aspects of him appealed to Herod.
An evangelistic program with its glamour,
advertisements that thrill, music that captivates
and compares with that which is heard in
public halls, these are the things which sometimes
we consider essential in a Church program.
This might be termed "Herodianism",
Jesus never performs miracles except when we
least expect them.

PRAYER PETITION:

May I seek Thee, not through curiosity, 0

Christ, but because there is in my life a need

MARCH 28

MATT. 27:15-26.

How easily the masses are swayed by a persistent
minority. Men in public office are the
victims of a few who may seek to work in a
sinister manner. Two or three, consecrated to
distinctive pursuits, can play havoc with
society. Jesus was a victim of such propaganda.
The twentieth verse indicates this. A few
"persuaded the multitudes that they should
ask for Barabbas, and destroy Jesus." In this
day let us think independently and act unitedly.
What a difficult thing to do.

PRAYER SUGGESTION:

Shall we, as members of our Church, or of
other Churches, enter together into united
prayer, this morning, that we may never be
swayed to do aught to displease or injure our
Lord and Savior.

MARCH 29

JOHN 19:1-6.

I can imagine that Jesus was able to endure
the physical torture he had to undergo, but
the scourge of words must have torn His
heart to shreds. Conceive, if you can, the
sarcasm and biting irony of "Hail, King of the

48

Jews." No sooner had the bitter words been said but "they struck him with their hands." Some murder with words. Such are more brutal than those who murder with an axe in cold blood. Great wars have been caused by little words. Christian! control those hastily spoken, bitterly expressed words.

PRAYER PETITION:

As we approach this period of agony in the life of Jesus, may we appreciate as never before His unspeakable suffering for us, His bitter humiliation, His never-dying love.

MARCH 30

LUKE 23 :26-32.

These are days when we should bear Jesus' cross with Him as did Simon of Cyrene. The cross, theologically, is symbolical of the sins of the world, which Jesus carries. As Christians, it is our responsibility to make the world cleaner and purer. Let us make His load lighter by telling others of His love and grace.

PRAYER PETITION:

May we not be like some, following afar off, as Thou approachest Calvary, but may we go beside Thee, bearing the cross along with Thee

MARCH 31

JOHN 19:16-24.

As you read of the Crucifixion, you and
others will be moved in different ways. One
catches one bit of truth, someone else another
thought. The soldiers cast lots for portions
of the Master's garments. To one was
given one, to another a different part. As
one studies the Crucifixion, he learns from it
just what he is able to understand. The marvel
of Jesus is that all can receive a distinct
blessing from Him.

PRAYER SUGGESTION:

Bow before the cross in prayer. Just kneel
in adoration before Him. He died for you,
for me.

APRIL 1

LUKE 19:29-41.

This is Palm Sunday. We read again the
familiar story of His entry into Jerusalem.
Also, our new ecclesiastical year begins today.
Let us pray that it may be "A new Triumphal
Entry of Christ into His Church. " We can
make His entry easier if we lay our pride, antagonisms
and respectable sins at His feet for
Him to tread upon.

PRAYER SUGGESTION:

Pray that as we enter upon this new year in the work of the Church, we may indeed invite the entrance of Jesus into our midst. Pray, too, that any palms of victory, which may be ours, shall be laid at His feet.

APRIL 2

JOHN 19:25-30.

I have often wondered just where the Church would have been had it not been for the devotion of her women. In fact, what would civilization amount to, were it not for womankind? Say what you will, moral tides are caused by the pure breezes of noble women. Humanity falls when women compromise with unrighteousness. At every Cross you will find a Mary.

PRAYER SUGGESTION:

There is in the life of each of us, some one woman who has been beside us, even beside our cross,-a mother probably, perhaps a wife, a sister or a daughter. Remember her in prayer today.

APRIL 3

MATT. 27:45-50.

"My God, my God, why hast thou forsaken me?" So cried Jesus out of the depths of His pain and sorrow. God always seems far away when life's clouds hang low. During physical ailments we become discouraged and take our eye off God. In those moments, faith must be enkindled. God is as near as our thoughts of Him. He always answers a sincere call.

PRAYER SUGGESTION:

Does God seem to have forsaken you? Just call upon Him now, at this moment, in a word of prayer. He will answer. Call and listen.

APRIL 4

LUKE 23:44-56.

"Father, into thy hands I commend my spirit". Psychologists inform us that immediately preceding death, all of the events of our lifetime pass before us in the twinkling of an eye. What remorse this panorama causes some, what elements of joy to others. How happy Jesus must have been, as the centurion said, "this was a righteous man". Death is not the end; it is merely handing the lamp of our Spirit to God.

PRAYER PETITION:

May I have such implicit faith in the Giver of my life that I shall at any moment be ready to return this life unto Him who gave it.

APRIL 5

MATT. 27:51-56.

All nature cries out at an injustice. The
universe is moral and quakes at a wrong.
Matthew, in his conception of what happened
following the death of Jesus, described what
thinkers have been able, only recently, to
embrace. He saw the moral laws of the universe.
You incur the hatred of Nature at every
violation of that which is true.

PRAYER PETITION:

All nature was angry when Thou didst hang
upon the tree. May we vehemently declare
our abhorrence of the daily Crucifixion of our
Christ.

APRIL 6

JOHN 19:31-42.
This is Good Friday. Our reading is not
chosen appropriately for the day, but we can
go back to preceding days and review
incidents pertaining to the death of our Lord.
Isn't it lamentable that those who love us fail
to express it until we are gone. Joseph of
Arimithea had been a secret disciple of Jesus.
Nicodemus dared come to Him only at night.
At HIs death, they came openly. Give to that
loved one the evidence of your love for him
now.

PRAYER SUGGESTION:

Pray that as your Savior enters into His
tomb, He may take with Him your sins
your evil impulses and unclean thoughts.

APRIL 7

MATT. 27:57-66.

The incidents in. this passage should be read
with care. The details are of utmost significance.
What we read tomorrow will be all
the more remarkable to our rationalistic minds
If we study today's details. The tomb was
"hewn out in the rock." Men recalled that
Jesus had said, "after three days I rise again,"
and they took precautions that this might not
be so. They had a "guard", and sealed the
tone. Only Omnipotent Power could break
through such a barrier.

PRAYER PETITION:

May we not, dear Jesus, so selfishly lock
Thee within our hearts, that others cannot see
that Thou art indeed a living Lord.

APRIL 8

MATT. 28:1-10.

No words can properly express the emotions
that should be in our souls today. You can
rightly estimate the warmth of your religious

54

experience by the impulses that sweep your soul throughout this day. Does the glorious fact of our Lord's resurrection mean something to you? Only angels can reveal the fact to you. These are thoughts from God testifying to the validity of inward things which the reason alone cannot affirm. Something is radically wrong with the heart which does not glow toward God today.

PRAYER SUGGESTION:

There is no need to suggest prayer to you today. Your hearts must needs cry aloud "Halellelujah, Christ arose!"

APRIL 9

MARK 16: 1- 11.

This morning we are making a study of the Resurrection from the view-point of Mark. Tomorrow and the next day we shall study the Luke and John accounts. On the essentials, we find each writer agreed although on minor details the human interest of the mind of each man expresses itself. The Bible becomes interesting only as we study it with care.

PRAYER PETITION:

After the exultation of the Easter Day, forbid that we lapse again into an indifference to Thy living reality.

APRIL 10

LUKE 24:1-12.

Luke was a physician. Naturally, his description of an event would signify medical knowledge. See if there is any revelation of his technical knowledge in this passage. Is it not marvelous that men of different race and intellect can all find something of winsome fascination about the Christ? Men may differ on man-made doctrines, but upon the salient facts of Him, all can be agreed.

PRAYER PETITION:

Often, dear Lord, when we see the glowing evidence of Thy reality, we are afraid. Grant us to know Thee as Thou art, a Risen Redeemer and Friend.

APRIL 11

JOHN 20:1-10.

These studies leading up to and concluding with the events succeeding Easter may have been a little more tedious than just one morning text. I trust that you have followed each suggestion and read each portion prayerfully. These four days of study have been more or less a duplication. However, the fact of the Resurrection should be branded upon our hearts and minds. Before your moment of prayer, close your eyes and review all the details pertaining to this passage.

PRAYER PETITION:

May we never echo the cry of Peter when
he said, "They have taken away the Lord."
Permit nothing to take Thee from me, I pray.

APRIL 12

JOHN 20:11-18.

The historical facts of this passage are of
much consequence. I shall add only a thought
or two to the apparent facts of the lesson. Mary
thoughts I seek to express in addition. Mary
discovered Jesus, her Risen Lord, through her
tears. Somehow, the great spiritual facts of
life comes to us often in this manner. Then,
too, she recognized Him only when He "saith
unto her, Mary." The personal element in the
Christian religion is marvelous. He knows
us by name.

PRAYER PETITION:

May we recognize Thy sweet, gentle voice
calling us by name,-perhaps even when we
would turn from Thee, looking for Thee elsewhere.

APRIL 13

MATT. 28:11-15.

Money can buy almost anything. Men can
always be found who will betray their Risen
Lord if only the price is great enough. It can
buy action but never a heart. Though the
soldiers spread propaganda of one sore I wonder
if in their hearts they were not convinced
of the Resurrection. In spite of what others
say or think, what their prestige may be, let us
never compromise with the facts of our faith.

PRAYER PETITION:

May there be nothing that ever comes to me
in life, powerful enough to cause me to deny
Thee.

APRIL 14

LUKE 24:13-27.

There is no passage on which I like to
preach more than this. The two men were
talking about Jesus as they walked home.
Perhaps that is why He "himself drew near."
Jesus rarely comes where folks do not at least
think of Him. Holden Eyes! That is the season
thy didn't know Him. There is nothing the
matter with the Christian Religion; our eyes
are holden. Again we find that Jesus revealed
Himself in the Home. Church is important,-but
prayer in the home reveals the Risen
Lord. Read the chapter with these suggestions
in mind.

PRAYER PETITION:

Thou art walking beside us all the way.
Open our eyes that we may see Thee.

APRIL 15

LUKE 24:28-35.

The danger of our studies together is that
they have dealt only with our own personal
development. Religion has a practical phase.
We must not only hear,-we must do as well.
These two men rose up "that very hour"
and went to tell others. Personal testimony
keeps the stream of our religious faith active.
Without an outlet, it becomes stagnant.

PRAYER SUGGESTION:

Pray that if, as a Church, we have felt Jesus
in our midst, we may go out, telling others
that we have seen the Risen Lord.

APRIL 16

LUKE 24:36-43.

In yesterday's thought we found that the
two men from Emmaus had testified positively,
"The Lord is risen indeed." It is easy enough
to dispute and argue the cardinal points of our
faith, but blessings come only as we believe.
Today we find that Jesus came into their very
midst. Why? Because they were talking and
thinking together about Him.

PRAYER SUGGESTION:

Offer a prayer that in our work together
we may so constantly talk of Him that He
Himself will stand in our midst.

APRIL 17

JOHN 20:19-25.

Closed doors are no barrier to Jesus when
He would come in. What a blessing to have had
Him come into their presence. But one was
missing! Thomas was away. Being practically
minded, perhaps he had no time to meditate
upon such intangibles as a Resurrected Lord.
So when He came, Thomas was not there. Oh!
let us not be so busy, so engrossed with this
world's affairs as "to be out" when He comes.

PRAYER SUGGESTION:

Meditate for a moment upon the last sentence
of the paragraph above. Then close your
eyes and offer it as your prayer.

APRIL 18

JOHN 20:26-29.

Jesus satisfies every type of faith. The
emotional soul receives from Him just what it
needs. The cold, calculating mind never need
go away from the Master without a blessing.
Only one thing is necessary,-"be not faithless

but believing." Belief builds facts. Belief
in Him brings the most philosophical to
say "My Lord and my God."

PRAYER PETITION:

I believe, 0 Lord. Increase Thou my faith
that I, too, may say, "My Lord and my God."

APRIL 19

JOHN 21:1-14.

The Scripture is so suggestive. Many precious
truths are in this passage for the believing
soul. Evidently the disciples had been fasting.
The Resurrected One ministered even to
physical needs. He suggested they break their
fast and partake with Him. Intimate fellowship
with Him feeds the soul more richly than
the externals of religion.

PRAYER SUGGESTION:

Christ will supply your physical needs. Take
them to Him as you would carry your desires
to an earthly parent.

APRIL 20

JOHN 21:15-24.

The obligation of love is responsibility.
With each answer to the question, "Lovest
Thou me?", Jesus gave Peter a duty to perform.

Perhaps that is why more of us are not
getting comfort and joy from our Christian
affiliations. We have failed to acquit a responsibility
commensurate with our love.

PRAYER SUGGESTION:

Ask God to reveal to you some very definite
work that you may do to feed His sheep and
thus prove your love for Him. Your answer
may come to you through very human mediums.
Listen! Watch!

APRIL 21

MATT. 28:16-20.

There is a human note here. The eleven
were on the mountain top with Jesus and they
worshipped Him; some doubted. To think,
that among the disciples, there were doubters.
Here we have the divine dynamic for missionary
endeavor,-"Go, and make disciples of all
nations." We believe in a Resurrected Savior to
the extent that we accept this. How humanly
tragic that "some doubted."

PRAYER SUGGESTION:

Pray for the missionary activities of our
Church and of the Church universal.

APRIL 22

MARK 16:9-20.

Here we have a fine summary of Jesus'
activities following the Resurrection. It tells
also of His glorification, "and sat down at
the right hand of God." The disciples continued
"and preached everywhere." They were
not alone for the Lord was with them. When
we labor for Him, we are never alone.

PRAYER PETITION:

I thank Thee that as I go about my task,
Thou art with me.

APRIL 23

LUKE 24:44-53.

The Ascension was a dramatic close to an
eventful life. No word of affirmation need be
said of this fact. In these verses the suggestion
comes that Jesus opened their mind, so
"that they might understand the Scriptures."
All of life He interpreted by the word. He
asked that we be His witnesses. Our lives and
thoughts bear witness of Him. "Pray what
is the gospel according to you?"

PRAYER PETITION:

Give me an understanding of the Scriptures
that I may know how to witness to their
truth.

APRIL 24

JOHN 20:30-31.

Haven't you often wondered what things
Jesus did other than those mentioned in the
New Testament? The thirtieth verse suggests
this thought. Also, the purpose of the Bible
is that we may have life. Life is an experience
begun with Christ and lasting through all
eternity.

PRAYER PETITION:

Grant me the assurance of eternal life, the
gift of Jesus Christ, the Son of God.

APRIL 25

LUKE 23:33-45.

We study this passage today because of its
religious practicability, not from a chronological
standpoint. "Father, forgive them, for
they know not what they do," is significant.
We never hate when we know a man.
Jesus knew this and forgave His enemies. Let
us do likewise. The Cross teaches this.

PRAYER PETITION:

Father, forgive those who would injure me.
They do not understand else they would do
differently.

APRIL 26

No man can serve two Masters. -MATT. 6:24.

This is a text which has often been quoted.
Abraham Lincoln made the thought of it the
basis of freeing the slave; "a house divided
against itself cannot stand." One cannot
serve evil and good at the same time. The
lesser good usually counteracts the greater.
Seemingly this is true [n the field of morals.

PRAYER PETITION:

Help me to know my Master. Him alone
I serve.

APRIL 27

Be ready to every good work. TITUS 3:1.

In all the activities, of life one should always be in an attitude of readiness. Business
does not come to an indolent or unprepared
man. Opportunities present themselves to the
man ready to receive them. If only we were
ready to do good. You may be called upon
today to do some deed of kindness. God is in
that call. Heed it.

PRAYER SUGGESTION:

If there has come to you a call to do some
good, ask God to prepare you to perform that
task.

APRIL 28

Acquaint now thyself with Him and be at peace. JOB: 22:21.

There is no time like the present moment. Most of us procrastinate. Some day we will pray, study the Bible, go to Church. E'er long we will be chained to habit and find ourselves unable to do the thing we would. "Now" is the time. Acquaintance with Him results in peace to our souls.

PRAYER PETITION:

Help me to know Thee now. I know so much about Thee, but I would know THEE.

APRIL 29

The temple of God is holy, which temple ye are. 1 COR. 3:17.

Our bodies are a vast and eternal cathedral. The contributions of ages are within us. We are not ourselves, we are thousands of others. Subdued lights, colored windows, muffled stillness, a grand organ,-all these contribute to our joy. Our lives are holy. God is within. Our bodies and minds are His. We are His Temples.

PRAYER PETITION:

Help me to make of my body a fit place to

66

enshrine its Builder and Maker.

APRIL 30

Ye know not what shall be on the morrow.
-JAMES 4:14.

Life is precariously uncertain. The man
who is killed today had no thought of
such a tragedy when he left his home this
morning. Life is eternal. There is no yesterday
or tomorrow. The present moment is
eternal. Rightly understood, there is no more
inspiring thought. Tomorrow shall take care
of itself, come what will, if only we hold the
hand of God today.

PRAYER PETITION:

May I put each day into Thy keeping. May
live it to the fullest, trusting to Thee for
tomorrow and its needs.

MAY 1

*He shall... save them because they trust
in Him.* -Ps. 37:40.

There is no greater thrill that comes into
my life than to have a little child leap from
an elevation into my arms. I love the chuckle
from his lips, the glow on his face as he leaps.
He trusts me. I would rather lose an arm than
lose his trust. So God shall save us because
we trust Him.

PRAYER PETITION:

I ask for deeper trust in Thee in all things.

MAY 2

Let us hold fast the profession of our faith
without wavering. -HEB. 10:23.

The facts of science have made religion
take more careful inventory of itself. Both
are builded on faith, but science seemingly
has more clearly defined its position. This and
many other things have often made us question
"the profession of our faith." Happy the soul
who trusts God even when he cannot see all
things. Anyone can doubt. Only the richly
endowed soul believes. "Let us hold fast."

PRAYER PETITION:

I have professed my faith in Thee. May
nothing turn me aside from faithfulness to this
profession.

MAY 3

His ears are open unto their prayers.
-1 PETER 3:12.

God is ever alert to the whispering of a
sincere heart. A man is not heard by his
vociferous prayer, nor his eloquence or repetitive
phrases, but rather by the unaffected sincerity
of his thought directed to God. Prayer need

not always be expressed to be heard. Prayer can be merely a wish to God. His ears are ever open to our prayers.

PRAYER SUGGESTION:

God knows what is upon your heart. Voice these desires to Him. His ears are open.

MAY 4

We have peace with God through our Lord Jesus Christ. -ROM. 5: 1.

There are many things the human heart desires. To name one as predominant in significance is seemingly presumptuous. On the cross preceding His death, Jesus left us "Peace." Perhaps He felt that of all human qualities this was most essential. Nations seek it. Humans fight for it. Strange, isn't it, but it can be had only "with God through our Lord Jesus Christ." The longer we live the more firmly we are convinced that this is the only means by which it might be had.

PRAYER PETITION:

"Take from our souls the strain and stress And let our ordered lives confess The beauty of Thy peace."

MAY 5

For the love of Christ constraineth us.
-2 COR. 5: 14.

Human passion is instinctive. It can express
itself in anger, hatred or other malicious
ways. The tendency of all is simply to "let
go." Religion tends to "hold back." The
text for this morning gives us the secret
of a strong and balanced life. Out of love for
Him and because of His abiding love for us
we are compelled to do away with the
perverted instincts common to mankind.
Humanity is clothed with divinity when we really
know Christ's love.

PRAYER PETITION:

When I would let my impulses or my passions
motivate my actions, then may I be
constrained by the love of Christ.

MAY 6

*The Lord is good to all; and His tender
mercies are over all His works.* -Ps. 145:9.

God's goodness is universal. We belittle
Him when we feel His providence is meted
out only to a select group. In His goodness
there is neither Jew nor Gentile, bond or free.
In our tolerance toward any people we reflect
the goodness of God. If He loves all, so must
we.

PRAYER PETITION:

Help me to know that Thou art God of all.
May I therefore be tolerant to all people.

MAY 7

When He giveth quietness, who then can
make trouble? -JOB. 34:29.

Divine quietness insures heavenly symphonies.
Nervous distraction, aimless expression
of energy tears the fabric of our souls. Our
high-strung dispositions make trouble makers
of us. Such are not malicious at heart, they
merely lack quietness. There is no poise which
is not born of God. Quietness is heavenly dew.

PRAYER PETITION:

May our lives be so pervaded with Thy
quietness, that nothing which man may do can
disturb us.

MAY 8

Honor all men. Love the brotherhood.
Fear God. Honor the king. -1 PETER 2:17.

One other morning we outlined a sermon
together. This text, according to the old
theories of Homiletics, has four points. You
can easily find them. This four-fold program of
life constitutes true Christian Citizenship. In
America, of course, we honor our

Government, not a king.

PRAYER PETITION:

Help us to adopt this text as the code of
our knighthood.

MAY 9

Christ is all, and in all. -COL. 3: 11.

How many of us believe the first part of
this text? I fear that most of us profess it,
but not many put it into life. There is no experience
in human endeavor akin to living, moving
and having our being in Christ. It is a
mystical relationship which strews life's
pathways with heavenly flowers.

PRAYER PETITION:

Help us to see the Christ in every person
whom we meet. Then shall we see the good
in each.

MAY 10

For to me to live is Christ, and to die is gain.
-PHIL. 1 :21.

Herein is the eternal philosophy of a genuine
Christian. "To live is Christ." All of life
subjected to His will; all activity charged by
Him,-that is life. Death is not the end; it
opens the portals of another life. What a

strange paradox; to live we must embody a life other than our own,-to die is to gain a richer, fuller life.

PRAYER SUGGESTION:

Can you truly pray that your life may be so hid in Him that for you to live is as if Christ lived in you? Can you pray that when you go to be with Him, that will be gain?

MAY 11

Follow peace with all men, and holiness, without which no man shall see the Lord. -HEB. 12:14.

Two things are essential if we "shall see the Lord." First, we must be at peace with all men. The responsibility is mutual. If another hates and afflicts us, we must, in spite of personal pride, be at peace with him. Second, holiness is a dominant requisite. To be holy is to conform perfectly to the will of God.

PRAYER PETITION:

Help me that in all my dealings with men, I may strive for peace and do only that which is good.

MAY 12

I can do all things through Christ which strengthen me. -PHIL. 4: 13.

This is a challenging text. It seems presumptuous. It involves a dynamic faith. If
we believed this there would not be the
multitudinous excuses expressed by most church
members as a legitimate reason for inactivity.
Laboring through Christ never wearies. Activity
through our own strength inevitably tires.
Whatever the problem confronting you today,
it can be done if executed through Him.

PRAYER PETITION:

In moments of weakness or when I face a
big task, may I know that if I rely upon Him,
Christ, Himself, will strengthen me.

MAY 13

He that planted the ear, shall he not hear?
He that formed the eye, shall he not see? -Ps.
94:9.

Most folks belittle God. They make Him
a victim of finite mind. Human laws often
subject God to their mandates. But God made
these minds which grope with eternal truths.
How can finiteness dictate to Infinity? If God
made our ears, surely He can hear the weakest
voice. If He formed the eye, He can see all
that is best for us.

PRAYER PETITION:

I am Thine, 0 God, Thou didst create my

every part. Surely then, Thou wilt continue
to care for me.

MAY 14

*Take heed, brethren, lest there be in any of
you an evil heart of unbelief, departing from
the living God.* -HEB. 3:12.

We have accepted without reservation that
doubts thought in sincerity are perfectly
Legitimate. So, some professors have taught.
"Unbelief" in the above text, comes from an evil
heart." Unbelief must come from a negative
faith; it cannot come from a heart beating in
love toward God. The doubting soul has
turned from the living God.

PRAYER PETITION:

Forbid, 0 Father, that any doubt or lack of
faith should turn me from the living God.

MAY 15

Son, go work today in my vineyard. -MATT.
21 :28.

Life is a stewardship. What we have, God
has but loaned us. Our stocks and bonds are
not ours; they are dependent upon the universe
holding together. The shrewdness and logic
with which a deal is consummated is made
possible because He gave us a mind with which
to work. Life is a vineyard staked out by God.

You labor today, as His workman, if you
believe God.

PRAYER SUGGESTION:

Pray, today, for this special spot in the vineyard of the Lord. Pray that our work' may
yield rich and abundant fruit. Pray, too, that
your task in the vineyard may be carefully performed so as to increase the fruitage.

MAY 16

*We know that all things work together for
good to them that love God.* -ROMANS 8:28.

Instinctively I believe the above. If there
never had been a text to express the thought,
I should have believed it anyway. One thing
is provisionary: "that we love God." If so,
then, ultimately, "all things will work
together for good." If not, then God is dead.
This is His universe and He dominates its laws.

PRAYER PETITION:

Grant to me sufficient faith to feel that God
is working His will always and that all things
are for a good purpose.

MAY 17

By the grace of God I am what I am. -1 COR.
I5: 10.

In all texts which we study, let us bear in
mind that one writer gave us the text. It
is his opinion' touched by the illumination of
God's Spirit. We, then, make the application
to our own lives. "What we are," states Paul,
"is through the favor of God." The secret of a
happy reconciliation to this fact hinges upon
the text of yesterday. If we love God then
what we are is the result of His grace.

PRAYER SUGGESTION:

Thank your God for the blessings and talents
which He has bestowed upon you.

MAY 18

*God is wise!' than men, and the weakness of
od is stronger than men.* -1 COR. 1: 2 5 .

Your happiness in life is dependent upon
your faith in God. Too often, a writer of
genius can make us doubt the wisdom of
God. We hold him to be stronger than God.
Meditated upon, is not such a .view ridiculous?
True, we cannot see God. We know His
reality only because of our faith. God's
weakest moment is stronger than the combined
efforts of the strength of men.

PRAYER PETITION:

We recognize that all true wisdom cometh
rom Thee. Help us to 'know wisdom from
knowledge; strength, as God giveth strength,

from mere physical prowess.

MAY 19

That Rock was Christ. -1 COR. 10:4.

Jesus once asked Peter, "Whom do men say
that I am?" After many personal theories,
Peter finally replied, "Thou art the Christ, the
Son of the Living God." Jesus said, "upon
this rock I will build my Church." In other
words, the Church is builded upon Christ. The
streams of living water come from this Rock.
At its side we are protected from the heat of
the sun, and the Juror of the storm. Our Rock
is Christ.

PRAYER PETITION:

"Rock of Ages, cleft for me, Let me Hide
myself in Thee."

MAY 20

In the beginning God..... -GEN. 1: 1.

The only portion of the first chapter of
Genesis of which I am rationally sure are these
four words. Schools and books have taught us
many things about evolution and other kindred
subjects which has made this knowledge
universal. The truth, God alone knows.
Whatever the process of life, this fact should
suffice,-"In the beginning God."

PRAYER PETITION:

May I never enter into any event of
significance until I have asked for Thy presence
with me. In the beginning of each day may
there always be God.

MAY 21

They that sow in tears shall reap in joy. -Ps.
126:5.

"Sow; and look onward, upward
Where the starry light appears;-
Where, in spite of coward doubting
Or your own hearts' trembling fears,
You shall reap in joy the harvest
You have sown today in tears."
PRAYER PETITION:

We thank Thee, Father, for the sweetening
influence of tears. The mint leaf, to be used,
must first be crushed. Perhaps, through
sorrow, Thou art enabling me to render fuller
service.

MAY 22

If God be for us, who can be against us?
-ROM. 8:31.

To be truly Christian invites unpopularity.
Too often this fact is taken as an occasion for
the expression of peculiarities. This should not

be so, but the Christian life is against the predominance of popular opinion. The favor of God makes unnecessary the plaudits of men. If we seek God first, real men will admire us. It matters not who may be against us if God is for us.

PRAYER PETITION:

I shall fear no man, a God, if Thou are beside me. The enmity of man is of little consequence as compared with the love of God.

MAY 23

Behold, I have refined thee, but not with silver; I have chosen thee in the furnace of affliction. -ISA. 48:10.

The happinesses of life do not call forth the real things of human experience. Through some strange workings of Providence, the furnace of affliction alone can temper our lives so as to make us strong. Most of us feel that money, with the comforts it can buy, can give us the things we need. Real worth is bought "not with silver," but is created through the tempering influences of life.

PRAYER PETITION:

We do not understand why we must suffer or why we must be tried in the furnace of affliction. But if I must be so refined, wilt Thou, a Lord, bring me through as pure gold.

MAY 24

And why call ye -me, Lord, Lord and do not
the things which I say? -LUKE 6:46.

Our faith involves two things-profession
and action. We must confess Him as Lord,
but this involves doing the things which He
says. We usually go to extremes. Either undue
emphasis is laid upon confession or upon
Christian deeds. A happy balance is the
desirable thing. It is obligatory to do the things
Jesus says if we have accepted Him as Lord.

PRAYER PETITION:

May my professian be a life to be lived, not
a mere repetition of words to be spoken.

MAY 25

So then everyone of us shall give account
of himself to God. -ROMANS 14:12.

Our actions are usually subjected to what
someone is going to say of us. We dress and
live in fear of the criticisms of others. Likewise we condemn and criticize other men. The
thought of the text is that men are not ac-
countable to us, nor we to them, for, "every
one of us shall give account....... to
God."

PRAYER PETITION:

Forbid that I shall be so busy watching the affairs of others that I shall cease to think of my own accountability of God.

MAY 26

Fore none of is liveth to himself and no man dieth to himself............ Whether we live, herefore, or die, we are the Lord's. -ROMANS 14:7,8.

A few days ago our thought implied that we should live solely for God irrespective of our social relationships. This morning's text, however, involves a social responsibility. In this day and age we are dependent upon others for all we have and are. Have you ever fully appreciated that your life is eternal; that whether you live or die, you are the Lord's?

PRAYER PETITION:

Help me to realize that I cannot live a selfish life, living as I choose. Thou hast granted this life unto me. It is a sacred trust. I am the Lord's.

MAY 27

Stand fast, therefore, in the liberty where-with Christ hath made us free, and be not en-tangled again with the yoke of bondage. -GAL. 5: 1.

Laws do not liberate. The mere fact that

a court has freed us of a charge, does not efface
the record from the books. Morally, we are
freed from the bondage of sin by Christ. Our
wrongs have been blotted from the memory
of God. O! that we believed this and never
again became entangled "with the yoke of
bondage."

PRAYER PETITION:

I thank Thee, God, that Thou didst free me
from a bondage to things which would have
destroyed my spiritual sense. May I be
sufficiently strong to hold fast to my freedom.

MAY 28

For if a man think himself to be something,
when he is nothing, he deceiveth himself. -GAL.
6:3.

The greatest proof, to me, of the inspiration
of the Bible is that it knows more about us and
touches us deeper than all other literature. This
depicts omniscience. How humanly true this
text is! .Most of us are conceited. When we
deny this, the shrewd mind knows we but
affirm it. Often the humblest, apologetic soul
is the most conceited. No one is deceived.
Mortals usually know. A man deceives only
himself.

PRAYER SUGGESTION.:

Thou knowest me as I am, 0 Lord. Forbid

that I should glory in myself when Thou canst
read my true worth.

MAY 29

*Prove all things; hold fast that which is
good.* -2 THESS. 5:21.

There is nothing in the Christian religion
which cannot stand the test of reason. The
greatest proof of real intellect, however, is the
realization that there are infinite truths in the
spiritual realm which cannot be thoroughly
comprehended by a finite mind. In all ages
there have been so many doctrines and theories
that it becomes difficult to choose the good
from the evil. We are bidden to prove all
things, to put them to the test of real values,
then to firmly cleave only to the good.

PRAYER PETITION:

Many things seem good, 0 God. Give me
the wisdom to choose wisely, and having selected
the good from the evil, may I hold
fast to that which is good.

MAY 30

*If in this life only we have hope in Christ,
we are of all men most miserable.* -1 COR.
15: 19.

Today our thoughts go to those who have
departed this life. Especially are we mindful

of those who gave their lives in service for their
Country. Soon, you and I will have gone
hence. Only the abiding characteristics of our
lives will be remembered. Character, alone,
endures. Let us form eternal habits before it
too late.

PRAYER PETITION:

As we think today, Thou Great Comforter,
of the dear ones who have left us, we realize
how true it is that without an assurance of a
life when we shall be reunited, we should be
of all men most miserable.

MAY 31

*Jesus Christ the same yesterday, and today
and forever.* -HEB. 13: 8.

The fact of Christ never changes. Men's
minds may be illuminated by intellectual or
spiritual development and their opinions of
Jesus change,-but He never does. Friends
come and go,-kingdoms rise and fall-human
love is dependent upon varied circumstances,
but Jesus is "the same, yesterday and today and
forever."

PRAYER PETITION:

We thank Thee that Thou are an unchangeable
Christ. Friends, loved ones, all my go,
but Thou art always the same.

JUNE 1

EXODUS 20:1-17.

For this month I have gathered some passages
of Scripture which I feel we should know as
Christians. You have doubtless been at a
home when the subject of Biblical knowledge
was discussed. Perhaps you felt humiliatingly
ignorant. A careful study this month,
(memorizing, at least, where familiar passages are
found). will tend to make you an educated
Christian. Learn again "The Commandments."
The abbreviated form is preferable for there is
much superfluous matter.

PRAYER PETITION:

Help me as I enter into this study of familiar
passages not to merely read them or, perhaps
memorize them, but may I make them a very
definite contribution to my living.

JUNE 2

PSALM 1.

In this Psalm we have a comparison between
the Righteous and the Wicked. The two ways
of life are carefully defined. One leads to a
very definite goal-the other, nowhere. The
Wicked "are like the chaff which the wind
driveth away." Could there be a worse hell
than to have no eternal identity? The righteous
endure like an oak tree, and always prosper.

Have your children, if there are any,
learn this Psalm.

PRAYER PETITION:

Grant us strength to withstand evil advice.
May we seek our counsel always in God's book
of the law. Then shall we become righteous
and endure forever.

JUNE 3

PSALM 8.

Herein is described God's glory and Man's
dignity. His glory is "upon the heavens."
The heavens are "the work of thy fingers."
Where, in poetry can one find such descriptive
power? Man is "but little lower than
the angels." He. has power over every living
thing. A study of this Psalm will teach the
omnipotence of God and the marvelous wonder
His creation,-Man.

PRAYER PETITION:

We bow before Thee in reverence, as we
see in all nature the magnificence of Thy creative
power. How excellent is Thy name, O Lord!

JUNE 4

PSALM 19.

I have before me three possible approaches to

a study of this Psalm. Each is by a renowned commentator. In reading each over several times, I have finally selected my own as the best for our study. Three great Facts are contained in it:

1. 	God 1-6.
2. 	Bible 7-11.
3. 	Man 12-14.

Each group of verses describes the subject I have suggested.

PRAYER SUGGESTION:

Offer sincerely as your prayer today the closing verse of the chapter.

JUNE 5

PSALM 23.

You will not need much memory work this morning. The Shepherd Psalm is known to all. If, perchance, you do not know it verbatim, permit no more time to elapse before memorizing it. We are His sheep because we are so foolish. Of all creatures, sheep are the most foolish. None need a shepherd as do these seemingly humble creatures. Come what will, His rod and staff will protect and find a way for us through life if only we place ourselves in His fold.

PRAYER PETITION:

This chapter has been the great comfort of

life. Write Thou each word upon my life that
I may never feel that I walk alone.

JUNE 6

PSALM 27.

The Psalmist here describes the joy of fearless
trust in God. Come what may-evildoers,
adversaries, war-one need not fear; "in the
covert of His tabernacle will He hide me. "Your
father and mother may forsake you, "then
Jehovah will take me up. "We find the secret of
this trust in the fourteenth verse, in the three
words, "wait for Jehovah."

PRAYER SUGGESTION:

Read this Psalm aloud and offer it unto God
as a prayer. It bespeaks a life of supreme trust
and fearlessness.

JUNE 7

PSALM 91.

I have already mentioned the text which I
consider carrying with it the greatest truth,
namely, Romans 8:28. This Psalm is my favorite
passage of Scripture. Many of you who
study it may recall my having read it during
your illness. Where can one find such comfort,
preceding, say, an operation as "He shall
cover thee with His feathers." "Thou shalt
not be afraid for the terror by night," or "For

He shall give his angles charge over thee....
They shall bear thee up in their hands."

PRAYER PETITION:

Thou art my refuge and my fortress: My
God, in Thee will I trust.

JUNE 8

PSALM 103.

This Psalm might well be studied at Thanksgiving. It is a song of Praise for the mercies
which the Lord has given us. One could feast
on the truths of this chapter for a month and
not become filled. Here you find the secret of
renewing your dissipated strength, having your
sins forgiven, God's loving kindness, pity, and
many other blessed and precious truths. Though
the task is great, do try to digest the contents
of this Psalm and establish them upon your
heart.

PRAYER SUGGESTION:

It has been suggested several times before
that we consider the blessings which come to
us. Read this Psalm, then pray, "Bless the
Lord, 0 my Soul, and forget not all His
benefits. "

JUNE 9

PSALM 119 :9.

Wherewithal shall a young man cleanse his way? By taking heed thereto according to Thy word.

There is no heritage as great as a working knowledge of the Bible. Parents cannot do better than instruct their children in it. Money cannot buy a clean life. Inward development is from spiritual truth, not material riches. Young man or woman, take heed!

PRAYER PETITION:

O wash me Thou, without, within. Cleanse me, God, through the medium of Thy Holy word.

JUNE 10

Again we have one of those passages which Immediately adjusts itself to homiletic treatment. God is the Keeper of His People. He:
1. Is ever alert.
"He, that keepth thee will not slumber.
2. Is Thy Protector.
"The sun shall not smite thee by day, nor the moon by night."
"Jehovah will keep thee from all evil."

3. Is an Enduring Companion.
"Jehovah will keep thy going out
and thy coming in from this day
forth and forevermore."

PRAYER PETITION:

God, Thou art indeed my ever-present help.
I thank Thee that Thou wilt never leave me
alone.

JUNE 11

ISAIAH 53.

Prophesies are difficult to understand. Practically
all that Jesus was and that occurred to
Him is described in this fifty-third chapter of
Isaiah. Some insist that the prophecy was
fulfilled in the period of Isaiah; others that Jesus
knew the prophecy and so lived as to work out
its details in His life. All these may have their
place as intellectual stimuli, but how much
better, to those of us who can never know, to
enjoy the fruits of positive fact-NOW.

PRAYER PETITION:

Our love for Christ Jesus increased as we
read again the supreme suffering and humiliation
which he here for us. We are bought
with the price of His life.

JUNE 12

ISAIAH 55.

Here we have the proof that the Messiah's
Kingdom shall ultimately triumph. The thirteenth
verse seems to indicate this. The chapter
was doubtless written in Palestine and contains
all the picturesqueness and imaginings of
the Orient. The eleventh verse is often quoted.
If it is true, we who preach should not worry
as we do. Where can one find finer poetry than
this, "the mountains and the hills shall break
forth before you into singing; and all the trees
of the field shall clap their hands"?

PRAYER PETITION:

We thank Thee for the beauty of Thy word.
We thank Thee that when we want to read
the finest literature, we can find it here in this
Book of Precious lessons.

JUNE 13

And she shall bring. forth a son, and thou
shalt call his name JESUS: for he shall save his
people from their sins. -MATT 1:21.

We look too lightly upon the subject of sin.
Pulpits are shying clear of the subject. Most
of us feel we are half ways decent and let it
go at that. All have sinned and unless God
through Christ has blotted out the transgressions
we are unsaved to that degree. Sin is as

vile in its respectability as in its ignominy.
Decent people need to be saved from their sins.
The revival of the future will have its
beginning here.

PRAYER PETITION:

We pray that we may feel that for salvation
from our sin we are dependent upon Jesus.
Each has sinned. Convict Thou us of our
sins.

JUNE 14

MATTHEW 5, 6, 7.

Though it might be impossible for you to
memorize all of the Sermon on the Mount, you
should know where it is found. The Beatitudes
should be memorized, also the Golden Rule. The
latter can be quoted from secular writings;
but rarely from the Bible. If you were to be
ignorant of all other Scripture except the Sermon
on the Mount, you would have a practical
working knowledge of all there is to
Christianity.

PRAYER SUGGESTION:

After reading the Sermon on the Mount, you
will be able to measure your life by the standards
which Christ gives you. Your prayer will
then be to make your life truer to His ideal
for you.

JUNE 15

MATTHEW 10:2-4.

As children, if we were taught the Scriptures,
we learned the names of the twelve
apostles. For your convenience I have suggested
devoting this morning toward the end
of learning their names. Your children will
raise you later if you teach them these things
now.

PRAYER PETITION:

Shall I, dear Jesus, find my name among
those of your faithful disciples

JUNE 16

*Whosoever therefore shall confess me before
men, him will I confess also before my Father
which is in heaven.*
*But whosoever shall deny me before men,
him will I also deny before My Father which is
in heaven.* -MATT. 10:32,33.

These verses are specific. There are no "ifs"
and "ands" about them. I would that they
were not in the Bible. If it were within my
power, the verses might be changed-a-but here
they are, said by Jesus, to be accepted or
rejected by mankind. They are not so much a
threat as an opportunity for an abundant life
to as many as will believe.

PRAYER SUGGESTION:

If you have never made a public confession
of your faith in Jesus, will you pray that you
may be led to do so now. If you have, pray
that you may never in life or word deny Him.

JUNE 17

MATTHEW 16:13-19.

We have made reference to this passage
heretofore. An intelligent Protestant should know
where it is' found and the details of the six
verses. The major point of difference between
Catholics and Protestants is found here. Peter's
marvelous confession is that which each
loving heart should make. Jesus wants a personal
confession, not what others may think
of Him.

PRAYER SUGGESTION:

I cannot suggest a prayer for you today.
You must state your own belief in Jesus. He is
asking! What is your answer?

JUNE 18

MATTHEW 22:35-40.
How simple the gospel is. One could easily
take a very few passages, thoroughly digest
them and have enough thought substance for
a lifetime. I sometimes think that if the Bible
were not so large, we might be more diligent

in our study of it. We like to see progress. Two
things upon which "the whole law hangeth,"
said Jesus, are first: Love toward God; the
her, Love toward man. How winsmoely
pie!

PRAYER PETITION:

May I live in my life the two great commandments
of Jesus, love toward God and love
toward my fellowmen.

JUNE 19

MATTHEW 25:1-13.

This is the parable of the Wise and Foolish
virgins. We should know immediately if asked,
just where it is found and the details of the
narrative. Too many of us, our spiritual lamps
going out, are asking of others, "give us your
oil; for our lamps are going out." Our lives
should be expectantly watchful "for ye know
not the day nor hour" when the bridegroom
cometh.

PRAYER PETITION:

I would be ready for Thy coming, Lord.
never face the tragedy of the closed

JUNE 20

MATTHEW 25:14-30.

What a marvelous chapter this is. Yesterday
we studied the parable of the Virgins; today
the Talents and tomorrow another interesting
portion from the same chapter. Science,
in Lamarch's law of "Use and Disuse" brings
out the thought of the talents. A wise and
proper investment of our talents, be they
spiritual or material, is essential to growth.

PRAYER PETITION:

What ever my talents, be they few or many,
they are God-given. May I be faithful in their
investment.

JUNE 21

MATTHEW 25 :31-46.

We never know when we are ministering to
God Himself. Perhaps you recall Tolstoi's
story "Where Love Is, There God Is." You
may recall that as the cobbler waited for the
coming of his Jesus, he ministered to the needy
who came his way. In so doing; he was granted
the joy of knowing that "Inasmuch as ye did
it unto one of the least of these, ye have done
it unto me."

PRAYER PETITION:

We pray Thee, that when an opportunity to
minister in Thy name comes to us, we may
avail ourselves of the privilege. We may find
that we have seen Him in the stranger whom

we fed.

JUNE 22

MATTHEW 28:18-20.

In a study of great passages to be studied carefully or memorized, "The Great Commission" must not be omitted. How can others know if we do not know? Half memorized texts are marks of careless souls. Especially should the nineteenth verse be memorized with exceedingly great care. A growing soul is a world visioned soul.

PRAYER SUGGESTION:

We should remember today those who have fulfilled this commission and are teaching all nations.

JUNE 23

MARK 10:13-16.

Great minds do not necessarily inherit the Kingdom of Heaven. Humility, purity, quiet simple minds, such as those of children-these alone enter therein. Jesus placed an eternal stamp upon the real meaning of childhood. How interestingly strange! The parent teaches the child-the child teaches the parent.

PRAYER PETITION:

Grant to us the simplicity and the purity of thought of the little child, that we may be fit for the kingdom of God.

JUNE 24

LUKE 9:23-25.

Each one of these three verses contains a precious gem of spiritual thought. In the first we are told the meaning of following Christ. We must assume a cross. Next we are told the most interesting paradox of' life, and then, one of the greatest truisms of life, that a man gains little "if he gain the whole world, and lose himself."

PRAYER PETITION:

I have sought all things for myself. Now may I be willing to lose my life in Thee, that may understand salvation.

JUNE 25

LUKE 15.

Jesus illustrates the Joy of Finding the Lost by three parables. We should ever remember where they are found as well as the substance of each parable. The following outline may aid you:
33.   The Parable of the Lost Sheep. 3 -7.
34.   The Parable of the Lost Coin. 8-10.
35.   The Parable of the Prodigal Son. 11-32.

PRAYER PETITION:

No matter how far we have strayed, Thou welcometh us back to Thyself. Even more, when we are lost, Thou seeketh us. Thank Thee for such love.

JUNE 26

JOHN 1:1-14.

Next to Tennyson's "Dora" and Poe's "The Bells", I believe the first five verses of this chapter are the most difficult to memorize. Try doing so. In theology this is called the Kenosis. The fourteenth verse, especially suggests the Kenosis, or "emptying himself." Though seemingly unimportant to the lay mind, in a list of great passages of Scripture, this one is invaluable.

PRAYER PETITION:

We are made to feel in this chapter today the oneness of Christ with God. We thank Thee that knowing the limitations of our human thinking, He took upon Himself such form as we would understand.

JUNE 27

JOHN 3:14-17.

More general than the twenty-third Psalm is ones knowledge of these verses, especially the sixteenth. Many attempt to quote it, but do so incorrectly. This is true more so of older people than it is of the younger. There should be no question as to what these verses say. Christianity will endure only as long as we believe and live the truth of this passage.

PRAYER PETITION:

This is the gospel in miniature. For its asurance, for the fact that it includes even me, thank Thee. We rejoice that God does not condemn but pardons and saves.

JUNE 28

JOHN 4:10, 13, 14.

"A well of water springing up unto eternal life." So spoke the Master of the Everlasting Life. How He used the homely things of life to illustrate heavenly things! A woman with a pitcher of water was taught in no uncertain way the fact of eternity. Often in the common things are found gems of everlasting lustre.

PRAYER PETITION

Thou hast pictured Thyself to us as the most essential elements in life--Bread, Light, Water. In Thee there *is* Life.

JUNE 29

JOHN 4:23-26.

The element of true worship seems to have lost its proper balance in our Churches today. Too often we come to hear the sermon or be thrilled by one of the many features, which, unfortunately are used as a bait to capture him who will be taught. Such church going is not worship. The secret is found in verse twenty-three.

PRAYER SUGGESTION:

Pray that we as a congregation may learn to come to the Church, not to be entertained or seen of men, but to worship in spirit and in truth.

JUNE 30

The Lord shall preserve thy going out and thy coming in from this time forth, and even for evermore. -PS. 121:8.

Rising from our knees this morning, following our period of devotion, life with its problems should have a new meaning for within our consciousness should be the thought, "The Lord shall preserve thy going out and thy coming in." Parents being separated for a while from their children should be mindful of this text. As we love Him so will the promise work out in our lives.

PRAYER SUGGESTION:

Use this text as a benediction upon your family circle this morning.

JULY 1

Fear thou not; for I am with thee. -ISA. 41:10.

As a young minister I had one or two sermons which I preached with great zest whenever called upon to go here or there. "The Fearless Life" with the above as the text was one of the sermons. I can still recall the outline and submit it to you for your thought:
1.   Fear Not to Live.
2.   Fear Not the Future.
3.   Fear Not to Die.

PRAYER PETITION

Grant me, the courage to live fearlessly. May I never compromise with that which is untrue but stand fearlessly for the right.

JULY 2

The Lord will not cast off forever. -LAM 3:31.

As we face with horror the sins of our lives we wonder how God, in His infinite Purity, could stoop to be personally interested in us. At best our lives are contaminated. What a marvelous promise that "the Lord will not cast if forever." The Divine heart always forgives, unless we fail to seek that grace.

PRAYER PETITION:

Even though friends or loved ones forsake
Thou wilt never leave me nor cast me from
Thee.

JULY 3

Do good, and lend, hoping for nothing again;
and your reward shall be great. -LUKE 6: 3 5.

This text, lighting upon a busy industrial
world, rebounds like a hammer against an anvil.
Our reaction is that the text is impractical and
obsolete. What would become of us if all
scripture were practical and fitted all of life's
circumstances. The text's idealism is inspiring.
It is not a mandate, simply a challenge to a
life seeking joy. "Do good hoping
for nothing... and your reward shall
be great."

PRAYER PETITION:

Help me, a Father, to give my gifts without
seeking returns of fame or gratitude for
myself.

JULY 4

The gift of God is eternal life through Jesus
Christ our Lord. -ROM. 6:23.

God gives color to the roses, a smile to a babe, the blush to a maid, purity to the snow, music to a stream; all of life is God's gift. None is so significant as the gift He gives through Jesus Christ. An eternal personality is God's greatest gift.

PRAYER PETITION:

We thank Thee, dear Father, for Thou hast given unto us the greatest gifts of life-the promise of eternal life and Thine only Son, even Jesus our Christ.

JULY 5

The Lord shall be thine everlasting light. -ISA. 60:20.

Life's paths carry us through many dark places. Enemies crouch in the darkness; unseen objects cause us to stumble and fall. The trusting soul, holding the lamp of truth, is given light for every pitfall. The Lord is an "Everlasting Light."

PRAYER PETITION:

In the midst of the dark moments which inevitably come, wilt Thou be unto me a Light.

JULY 6

Certainly I will be with thee. -Ex. 3: 12.

God's promise to the people of Israel is as true today as it was in the days of the Exodus. His only provision is that we obey His mandates. There is a note of positiveness in the text, as if God, anticipating our doubts, seeks to allay them by saying "Certainly I will be with thee."

PRAYER PETITION:

We thank Thee for the certainty of Thy presence with us.

JULY 7

Thou shalt guide me with thy counsel, and afterward receive me to glory. -PS. 73 :24.

In travelling to Europe, we seek counselor advice from our Consul. He arranges the passports and tells us how best to adjust ourselves in other lands. Then, after we have crossed the ocean, we are received on the other side and are at home according to our ability to carry out our Consul's suggestions. Our Divine Counsellor not only counsels us here but receives us there.

PRAYER PETITION:

Help me to understand when 'Thou wouldst guide me with Thy counsel. I can hear Thee if only I know how to listen.

JULY 8

There is a friend that sticketh closer than a brother. -PROV. 18 :24.

There are many attributes of God. All are marvelous. To me the fact of His Father-hood is chief, though I never knew a human father. Perhaps we appreciate most the things we have never had. Preachers have many wonderful acquaintenances, but because of their transciency, few friends. Furthermore, speaking again personally, I have never had a brother. However, the text makes a profound impression on me. "There is a friend that sticketh closer than a brother."

PRAYER PETITION:

Thou hast given unto us sweet, human relationships. But truer even than the loyalty of a brother, is that of our Friend.

JULY 9

If ye seek him, he will be found of you. -2 CHRON. 15:2.

Here we have the Philosophy of Religion. God is usually pictured as wooing us to Him. We can live as we will, ultimately His grace will find us. This text places the responsibility where it ought to be. Having taken the initiative and sought Him, then you can find Him. Lees go half way with God.

PRAYER PETITION:

We thank Thee that Thou dost never hide
Thyself from us. If we but seek Thee, Thou
canst always be found. May we not wait for
Thee to come to us.

JULY 10

And I will be a Father unto you, and ye
shall be my sons and daughters. -2 COR. 6: 18.

In a time of sorrow this text will bring
much comfort. If you have lost an earthly
parent God promises to "be a Father unto
you." He does not bear this relationship to
you merely in an impersonal sense but you shall
be His son or daughter. Hold tight to this
promise.

PRAYER SUGGESTION:

Just as you, as son or daughter, confide in
your parent, and ask him for what you want,
even more frankly go to your Great Father.

JULY 11

A little leaven leaventh the whole lump.
- GAL. 5:9

This text in modern terminology simply
means that a small bit of yeast raises the whole
loaf of bread. So a man's individual life exerts
a mighty influence upon the whole mass of

society. Let us see to it that the necessary vitality is within the substance of our life.

PRAYER SUGGESTION:

Your prayers may be the leaven that shall bring about a revival within our church. Pray!

JULY 12

As we have therefore opportunity, let us do good unto all men. -GAL. 6: 10.

Opportunities have much of Providence in them. Often we create our opportunities. There should be no discrimination in our service. We can't choose whom we will serve. The text is specific, "do good unto all men."

PRAYER SUGGESTION:

A great opportunity to do good comes through our prayers. Today pray for others.

JULY 13

The Lord hath dealth bountifully with thee. -Ps. 116:7.

There are few who will read this text this morning who cannot say "amen" to it. Perhaps, if you feel a right to question His goodness, you have not always done your part in being obedient to Him. God tests us with poverty and with riches. There are bounties in poverty and poverty in riches. Let him who understands, take heed.

PRAYER SUGGESTION:

It is well that we should pause frequently to "count our many blessings." Name them one by one in your prayer today.

JULY 14

Let them also that love Thy Name be joyful in Thee. -Ps. 5: 11.

Dr. George L. Robinson, of McCormick Theological Seminary, famous as a writer and a professor, determined to give his heart to God and enter the ministry because of the joy he saw on the countenance of a minister. Long-faced Christianity has long ago been expelled. Those of us who love God must be joyful not only in Him but in our relationships one with another.

PRAYER PETITION:

I would be a cheerful Christian. May I seek joy, not merely pleasure.

JULY 15

Make the voice of His praise to be heard. -Ps. 66:8.

God's goodness hath been great to thee,

Let never day nor night unhallowed pass,
But still remember what the Lord hath done.
-Shakespeare

PRAYER SUGGESTION:

God appreciates gratitude. Let us make
Him glad today as we use our moment of
prayer to praise Him.

JULY 16

He will be our guide even unto death. -Ps.
48:1,4.

The text we studied a few days ago to the
effect that "There is a friend that sticketh
closer than a brother" is a companion text to
this one. Through all the devious paths of life
He is our guide. We may be called to pass
through the valley of the shadow-still He is
our guide. His guidance does not end at our
death, but then He assumes more complete
charge, guiding our bark across the sea into that
land which is otherwheres.

PRAYER SUGGESTION:

We fear death, 0 God, but give us the courage
to face all things, even death, bravely, with
Thee as our guide.

JULY 17

*God forbid that I should sin in ceasing to
pray.* -1 SAMUEL 12:23.

Failure to pray is certainly a sin. If a man professes to love his wife and never tells her so, we have a right to question that love. Prayer is not mere eloquence raised to a preacher's tone, it is the stammering expression of our love toward God expressed in the language of our own soul.

PRAYER PETITION:

Thank Thee, Christ Jesus, for teaching us to pray. It is a privilege to come to Thee in prayer. May I never lose my resolve to make prayer a fixed habit in my life.

JULY 18

Seek ye first the Kingdom of God, and Ill! righteousness; and all these things shall be added unto you. -MATT. 6:33.

Too often in religious matters we neglect to place the emphasis where it ought to be. WI' seek education and culture, social standing and other things. If God were the first we sought, then all the events of life would be properly sorted out for us: In their proper relationship the things that are needful come to us, if God be sought first.

PRAYER PETITION:

Often we seek first material blessings, our Father. Help us out of our devotion to Thee, without thought of gain, to put first things first.

JULY 19

The Lord is good ... to the soul that seeketh
Him. -LAM. 3:25.

There is so little of devotional value that
can be written of texts that are so obvious as
this one. The retroaction of seeking Him is
His goodness. It is obvious, from the standpoint of common sense, that, unless I go to the
store for bread and make known my desire, the
the baker cannot supply my need. If we seek
God, He can easily be found and then will
willingly manifest His goodness.

PRAYER PETITION:

We praise Thee for Thy goodness. We thank
Thee that Thou wilt never reject us if we
seek Thee honestly.

JULY 20

Whatsoever thou wilt ask of God, God will
give it to Thee. -JOHN 11:22.

There need be no word on prayer other than
that which is found in this text. It is short,
positive and right to the point. Oh! to approach
God in such faith. Could there be any question
as to His giving us the things we desire
if we asked positively. Prayer is always answered
one way or another. Perhaps the answer
would be more immediate if you came in
he attitude suggested by this text.

114

PRAYER SUGGESTION:

There is probably some one thing which you
very much desire. Go to God, believing that
He will answer.

JULY 21

He knoweth our frame; He remembereth
that we are dust. -PS.103:14.

God is our Creator. As an automobile engineer
knows all the parts that have into the
construction of a new car, so God knows all
about us. He realizes that we are mere dust
breathed upon by the Divine. This should not
give us occasion for moral laxity, even though
God might understand our human frailties.
Though humans may misunderstand, God
knows every detail about us.

PRAYER PETITION:

Thou dost always understand our shortcomings
and wilt pardon us for Thou knowest
the very weakness of our frame.

JULY 22

God resisteth the proud, but giveth grace
unto the humble. -JAMES 4:6.

Certain things have no place in the Kingdom
of God. Pride is one of them. We have
no legitimate reason for pride. We, of ourselves,

have done nothing which is attributed
to us. The strength, ability and opportunity
came from God.
He that is down need fear no fall
He that is low no pride
He that is humble ever shall
Have God to be his guide.
-Bunyan

PRAYER PETITION:

It is so difficult to be truly humble. 0
God, we so often stand aside from Thee and
from our fellowmen because we are so proud.
Teach us humility.

JULY 23

*If children, then heirs; heirs of God, and
joint heirs with Christ.* -ROM. 8:17.

There are three steps necessary to gain the
heritage that is ours in Christianity. Except
we become as little children, we cannot see
the Kingdom. Then it follows that we become
heirs of God and jointly so with Christ.
No will is so marvelous as the one which leaves
unto us the estate of God's Kingdom.

PRAYER PETITION:

We rejoice to claim our kinship with Jesus
Christ as Thy child. Help us to truly value
the incomparable riches which are our
heritage.

JULY 24

Hear, O Lord, when I cry with my voice. -PS. 27:7.

Seemingly there are more texts on prayer
in these studies than on any other subject.
Well might this be the case. Contact with
God is. possible only through prayer. Any
other method is impersonal and indefinite. Talk
to a man and you know him. Read of him
and your knowledge is second hand. Cry with
your voice or speak with your heart-He hears.

PRAYER SUGGESTION:

It may be you have never gone to God with
cry in your voice and you have wondered
why your prayers were not answered. Let God
know something of the depth and sincerity of
your trust in Him as you pray today.

JULY 25

... Called out of darkness into his marvelous light. -1 PETER 2:9.

There is no darkness greater than that of a
soul without Light. There are different types of
religion just as there are degrees of illumination.
Electric power gives more light than
candles. So Jesus gives more Light than Confucius
or Buddha. Christ is a "marvelous
Light."

PRAYER PETITION:

Help me to go into the dark places of life,
glowing and shining as a ray radiated out into
the world from the Marvelous Light.

JULY 26

*As the Father hath loved me, so have I loved
you: continue ye in my love.* -JOHN 15:9.

Jesus seemed anxiously concerned lest His
disciples not continue in the brotherly love
which He had taught. This suggestion occurs
many times. I wonder if He foresaw the
discordancies that sometimes develop between
Christian brethren. The most powerful church
of the future is that one which continues in
His love.

PRAYER SUGGESTION:

This was Jesus' commission to His disciples.
Pray that we, as His followers, shall continue
in love one toward another and toward Him.

JULY 27

*Awake thou that sleepest, and arise from the
dead, and Christ shall give thee light.* -EPH.
5: 14.

We must be careful not to remove text
from their original setting. Too often we are
prone to make personal application, forgetting

that the text had one particular people in mind. However, it does seem as if the text were a challenge to the modern church member. I leave it to you to read the text again. Christ alone can give such light.

PRAYER SUGGESTION:
Though not physically dead, many of us arc spiritually so. Shall we pray together that there may come to our Church a real spiritual Resurrection and that we shall show forth the light which He will give?

JULY 28

I am poor and needy; yet the Lord thinketh upon me. -PS. 40:17.

The text could read "I am rich and bountifully supplied; yet the Lord thinketh upon me." The Psalmist does not necessarily depict a financial class; he is dealing with the merit of the spirit. What ever our condition "the Lord thinketh upon me." Jesus, later, you re-call, said, "Blessed are the poor in spirit."

PRAYER PETITION:

Although I may be richly blessed with this world's goods, yet I am, indeed, poor and needy, unless Thou art with me.

JULY 29

I will put my spirit within you. -EZEK. 36:27.

The difference between a brute and a human is God's spirit. God breathed into us His spirit. As members of a Church your financial rating rank in a community is not of greatest significance. Your value to God depends upon the reality of His spirit within you.

PRAYER PETITION

Thou hast truly breathed Thy spirit into each of us. How often we belie Thy presence in our lives! May we realize that others see Thee through us.

JULY 30

God shall wipe away all tears from their eyes. -REV. 21 :4.

Here we have a text from the hardest book in the Bible. It gives us a portion of a picture of heaven. All of life's sorrows shall be wiped away and "God shall wipe away all tears from their eyes." Heaven is infinitely greater than our highest opinion of it. Too often we make heaven an ideal earth. God alone knows what He has prepared for us. I am content to follow Him here knowing then He will lead me there.

PRAYER SUGGESTION:

Remember today any of your dear ones and members of our church who have had sorrows during the past month.

JULY 31

They that wait upon the Lord shall renew their strength. -ISA. 40:31.

One must not be fanatical in his religious experience. In reading a text such as this we might be inclined to feel that sanatoriums were no longer of any use. Perhaps they would be less popular if we realized that the renewing of strength was born through the nature of the spirit and not out of pill boxes.

PRAYER PETITION:

Often, Father, we do not wait with patience for Thee to answer prayer. Teach us to learn the lesson of waiting. In patience is there strength.

AUGUST 1

When he hath tried me, I shall come forth as gold. -JOB 23: 10.

Job suffered much humiliation for his faith. suppress him, his faith triumphed. God subjects us to life's trials to see whether we are worthy of wearing a crown. The afflictions of life burn out the dross and the abiding things "come forth as gold."

PRAYER PETITION:

May I have such implicit faith in my trust

in God that I shall know that no matter the afflictions which come, nothing can prevent my coming through as gold.

AUGUST 2

Surely goodness and mercy shall follow me all the days of my life. -PS. 23 :6.

When we make the Lord our Shepherd, then the promise of the above text can be depended upon. This text is like my favorite found in Romans 8:28. Things work together for good only when we love God. Likewise the promise of this text can be depended upon when "the Lord is my Shepherd."

PRAYER PETITION:

We thank Thee for this glad song of faith. May we remember always that no matter into what pastures we are led, goodness and mercy are ever following.

AUGUST 3

I am the Light of the World; he that followeth me shall not walk in darkness. -JOHN 8:12.

We began this book with a text from the Psalmist. 'Thy word is a Lamp unto my feet and a Light unto my path." This text is similiar except that it refers to Christ. Nothing can be added to or taken from the text. It is self-explanatory.

We dislike darkness and yet how often we refuse to turn from it to the glorious Light. Grant me 'to see Thee and follow Thee, Thou Light of the World.

AUGUST 4

Even so the tongue is a little member and boasteth great things. Behold, how great a matter a little fire kindleth! -JAMES 3: 5.

Forest fires are a great menace. No fire seems more devastating. Only one is greater- the one caused by the tongue. No two people can relate the same story. Begin a story and pass it around the room by word of mouth and the entire subject will be changed by the time it gets back to the center of the ring. Tongues are dangerous members. Keep them quiet or they will cause fires which several generations cannot fully extinguish.

PRAYER SUGGESTION:

Pray that if through you, a fire has been kindled, somehow the waters of God's love and kindness may go before, making impossible further spreading of the flames.

AUGUST 5

And whatsoever ye do, do it heartily, as to the Lord, and not unto men. -COL. 3:23.

There has always been a tendency to please men. Those who pray in public sometimes think of the effect of the words upon men and not their power with God. This is a human trait and sometimes excusable. If we conceive life as eternal then our every act would be done "heartily as to the Lord."

PRAYER PETITION:

I pray that Thou wilt take from me the desire to be a "men-pleaser." May I today do each act, think each thought, heartily, as to the Lord.

AUGUST 6

The mercy of the Lord is from everlasting to everlasting unto them that fear him. -PS. 103:17.

God's blessings to us are usually provisionary. It is well that they are, otherwise we would loon lose our respect for Him. Respect gone -love soon disappears. God's mercy is Everlasting if we fear Him. Likewise good comes to us if we love Him. "God's Provisionary Blessings" might make an excellent topic for sermon.

PRAYER PETITION:

Grant that I may not become so sure of Thine everlasting mercy, that I shall cease to bow in awe and reverence before Thee.

AUGUST 7

I am not ashamed of the gospel of Christ:
for it is the power of God unto salvation to
every one that believeth. -ROM. 1: 16.

This is one of the grand texts of the ages.
It has been the favorite of many great preachers
in the past. Can we say the first clause
without reluctance? Seemingly some are afraid
to admit their faith in the gospel. Again we
have the provision we studied about yesterday.
The gospel is "the power of God...to
everyone that believeth."

PRAYER PETITION:

Keep us from ever being ashamed to acknowledge
our allegiance to the Great King of Kings.

AUGUST 8

Fathers, provoke not your children to anger,
lest they be discouraged. -COL. 3 :21.

Somewhere Jesus said regarding those who
provoke their children to wrath, that it were
better than a millstone be hanged about their
necks. We all admit this, but there are many
ways which we as parents provoke each day of
our lives. Think of half a dozen ways in
which you do this and take the things to God
in prayer, asking that He blot them out of
your life.

PRAYER PETITION:

Make us to be more thoughtful as to what
our influences may be upon the little ones in
our homes, or with whom we come in contact.

AUGUST 9

*Did not our heart burn within us, while He
talked with us by the way? -LUKE 24:32.*

I fear that many of us have lost much of the
thrill of religion. The reason for this is that
the minister, a member, or perhaps the church,
displeased us and we became disinterested.
In other words, we crucify Christ again,
because of some human's injustice. After
all, our interest should be in Christ. Our
hearts will glow within us through talking
about Him. Hearts are never heavy when we
think of God. Go to Church and talk with
Him. That is real worship.

PRAYER PETITION:

Enkindle within us a burning zeal for Jesus
Christ. We ourselves can light what may be
dying embers by making Him the keynote of
our every-day living.

AUGUST 10

*Every good gift and every precious gift is
from above. -JAS. 1: 17.*

After you hear people ask whether sin originated
with God or is permitted to exist by Him.
It is akin to the question children ask as to
why God created snakes. I like to think that
the text of the morning explains much of the
dilemma. If the text is true, then perhaps the
opposite is true, that evil things come from
below. Without evil, perhaps we could not
appreciate the good. God's Providence can
convert every sin and wrong into a marvelous
blessing.

PRAYER PETITION:

Help me to receive gratefully the good gifts
which come from Thee, and to reject the evil
which would creep into my life.

AUGUST 11

*Hast thou faith.? Have it to thyself before
God.* -ROM. 14:22.

This text seems diametrical to many that we
have studied. Should a man's faith be kept
to himself and his God? Possibly Paul had in
mind the Publican and the Pharisee. The
Pharisee knew he was a good man, and this
knowledge made him a sinner. If we express too
loudly our faith, men might begin to question
it. A sincere faith will soon speak louder than
anything we can ever say about it.
PRAYER PETITION:
Grant me a quiet faith. May I not seek to
convince others of my goodness, only to prove

myself before Thee.

AUGUST 12

He forgave ... their iniquity. -Ps. 78:38.

I like short simple texts. They give no
opportunity for doubts and questionings. We
simply know that they are. Forgiveness is one
of God's greatest gifts to man. When we are
forgiven, all record of the wrong is blotted
out. Our sins are removed as far as the east
is from the west. They are even removed from
the mind of God. If the fact were proven untrue,
what a marvelous comfort to believe it
anyway.

PRAYER SUGGESTION:

Today shall we stop again to recognize our
sins, little though they may seem to us, and
ask for His forgiveness.

AUGUST 13

I have loved thee with an everlasting love.
-JER. 31:3.

Sometimes we become removed from the
tender intimacy with God that should characterize Christians. Then it is, that we fail to
fully appreciate His Love. When friends. desert
us and loved ones die and leave us, IS It
not marvelous to recall that He loves us with
an everlasting love?

128

PRAYER PETITION:

"O Love, that will not let me go, I rest my
weary soul in Thee."

AUGUST 14

Ask thy Father and He will show thee.
-DEUT. 32:7.

This text sounds like a mother speaking to
a ten year old boy. Instead it is an admonition
for us to go to God our Father and He
will show us. Again this is provisionary.
According to our faith in God as a Father, can
we expect Him to show us.

PRAYER PETITION:

Teach us to approach Thee confidently and
trustingly, in the simple faith of a child
seeking His parent.

AUGUST 15

He forgetteth not the cry of the humble. -PS.
9: 12.

God is not an aristocrat.
He makes no discrimination between persons.
The timid, humble soul is heard as quickly
as the eloquent voice of an influential statesman.

PRAYER PETITION:

"Bowed in lowliness of mind
I make my humble wishes known
I only ask a will resigned
0, Father, to Thine own."

AUGUST 16

*He that hath My commandments and keepeth
them, loveth me.* -JOHN 14:21.

The trouble with Christians is not that they
do not know the right, but they fail to do the
right. His Commandments are pretty firmly
installed into the hearts of men. We merely
fail to keep them. You can test your love for
Christ by keeping His Commandments.

PRAYER PETITION:

How keenly Thou must feel our neglect to
prove our love by keeping Thy Commandments.
Forgive, Father, for we do love Thee,
and shall strive to do as Thou biddest.

AUGUST 17

Thy face, Lord, will I seek. -PS. 27:8.

No man has ever seen God's face. To seek
His face is an eternal quest. The mere fact
that our quest will never be rewarded in this
life should not deter us; think of the marvelous
development we will make in seeking to find.
Real joy is not in realization, but in anticipation.

PRAYER PETITION:

Perhaps, Father, we see Thee as we serve.
We may not know when we are face to face
with Thee. Give us spiritual sight.

AUGUST 18

Let not the sun go down upon your wrath.
-EPH. 4:26.

This was a text which my mother taught
me as a child. In spite of my wickedness, she
would never let me go to sleep until she had
forgiven me. Oh! that we were all as punctilious.
Anger generates a poison which can kill.
Let us put this text into action and see if we
do not feel better in every way.

PRAYER SUGGESTION:

If there is someone with whom you are
wrathful, try today to settle the matter,
lovingly. Then pray. Perhaps that is why your
prayers are not being answered.

AUGUST 19

They shall prosper that love thee. -PS. 122:
6.

This text will be questioned by many of
you. You are reminded of the many who have
gained riches and never even thought of God.
Likewise it is true that some who love Him

most have prospered least. Riches alone do not indicate prosperity. Some of the wealthiest are the poorest. True love toward God gives eternal prosperity.

PRAYER PETITION:

Grant us to know the real riches of life. May we realize that the greatest prosperity comes through the joy of a life well spent.

AUGUST 20

I press toward the mark for the prize of the high calling of God in Christ Jesus. -PHIL. 3: 14.

It is interesting to note how many times Paul makes reference to the games of his day. "A cloud of witnesses" refers to the bleachers. The prize of this text pertains to the reward of the victor. The Christian is ever in a race endeavoring to win the prize of a life hid in God through Christ Jesus.

PRAYER PETITION:

May I never cease to run onward toward the goal of oneness with God, through Christ Jesus,

AUGUST 21

I was brought low, and He helped me. -PS. 116:6.

The proud in spirit are not blessed of God.
We find that the haughty and domineering
are not even respected by their fellowmen. As
we are brought low, God helps us. Jesus came
not to save the conceited, but the needy.

PRAYER PETITION:

The lesson of humility is so hard to learn,
Father. If need be, bring me low, that I may
be lifted by Thee.

AUGUST 22

*Whatsoever we ask, we know that we haw
the petitions.* -1 JOHN 5:15.

The secret of prayer is the knowledge that
we already have the petition for which we
have asked. Acting upon their affirmative answer
gives us much joy. Approaching Him,
tremulously hesitant, does not enable God to
bless us as He would if our Faith were strong
enough.

PRAYER SUGGESTION:

Just pray and know that God hears. Ask
whatsoever you would.

AUGUST 23

Come unto Me and I will give thee rest.
-MATT. 11:28.

Jesus preached to a tired people. Many were in bondage. They were weary of governments and religions. The times were akin to ours. Churches beckon us and "isms" call, but men heed them not. However, men do desire Christ, unadorned by the many frills of modern culture. He gives rest.

PRAYER PETITION:

We become so weary, Lord. If we but knew that the sweetest rest is found when we lean back into the everlasting arms.

AUGUST 24

*Thy prayers and thine alms are come up ...
before God.* -ACTS 10:4.

God hears the slightest whisper of the soul and sees the smallest gift; Let us live in such intimate communion with Him as to make our gifts known to Him. Too many seek notoriety for their giving. Prayers and gifts are most forceful when offered to God or in His name.

PRAYER PETITION:

Take from our hearts any desire to have our alms seen of men. May we offer our prayers and gifts as if unto Thee alone.

AUGUST 25

He that wavereth is like a wave of the sea
driven with the wind and tossed. -JAMES 1:6.

Stubborn men are usually weak men. They
are stubborn because they have few qualities
of reasoning power. In pleading for firmness
I do not mean stubbornness. Religiously and
otherwise, some men waver like the waves of
the sea. Winds of public opinion toss men
about aimlessly. These are days when the bark
of firm religious faith must ride the crest of
every wave of doubt.

PRAYER PETITION:

O God, give us strength to be determined in
our faith. May no new theory or doubt come
to toss us about like a wave on a troubled sea.

AUGUST 26

Confess your faults one to another, and pray
one for another. -JAMES 5: 16.

Great men admit their faults; weak men
hide them. Confession of them can be affected
goodness; only in prayer for one another can
good be accomplished. When differences arise,
there is usually mutual wrong; prayer plus
confession is a sure antidote.

PRAYER SUGGESTION:

Shall we not this morning pray for other ,
especially for those others against whom we
know we have committed an injustice? Are
we strong enough to both pray and confess?

AUGUST 27

Love as brethren, be pitiful, be courteous.
-PETER 3:8.

Pity of the right sort is akin to godliness.
Courtesy lifts pity to the dignity of respect.
Love unites souls into a harmonious
friendship. Courteously pitying, courteously
loving, unites men as brethren.

PRAYER SUGGESTION:

Pray that we may learn to be kindly courteous.
May we no longer hold ourselves aloof
but seek to be friendly.

AUGUST 28

*If any man suffer as a Christian, let him not
be ashamed.* -1 PET. 4: 16.

Too often Christianity is pictured as an easy
life. It ceases to be attractive when it loses its
problems and obstacles. We should not seek
suffering, but it does sweeten life as happiness
never can. Christian suffering develops
Christian living.

PRAYER PETITION:

136

There come times when the Christian life
is ridiculed. Then may I prove my willingness
to suffer as a Christian. May I never be
ashamed to say "I am a Christian."

AUGUST 29

*Whoso stoppeth his ears at the cry of the
poor, he also shall cry himself, but shall not be
heard.* -PROV. 21:13.

The apt thing can always be found in Proverbs.
Caring for the needy is but a safeguard
for ourselves. Failure to heed their cry will
ultimately bring need to our own doors, and
then when we cry, no one will hear. The universe
pays us back with whatever we have invested
in it.

PRAYER PETITION:

Help me to give a sympathetic, generous
heart. May I never be so engrossed in caring
for my needs, that I shall forget him who is
less fortunate.

AUGUST 30

*If ye love them which love you, what
reward have ye?* -MATT. 5:46.

There is no real joy in giving gifts to those
from whom we know we shall receive.
The test of love is not the return of our affection,
but rather its embrace of those we know

do not like us. Real reward comes from lack of reward.

PRAYER PETITION:

Teach me to love those whom it is difficult for me to love.

AUGUST 31

Agree with thy adversary quickly, whiles thou art in. the way with him. -MATT. 5:25.

Personal rights breed more discordancies than any element in human relationships. To a real Christian, righteous indignation, personal rights and a "case" have no place. Measured rights are unchristian. The greatest happiness comes, according to the text, in agreeing with those who seek their own way.

PRAYER SUGGESTION:

Pray, that if you wilfully seek your own way in matters that are of more than personal interest, you may learn the Christian attitude of "agreeing with your adversary."

SEPTEMBER 1

Who can say, I have made my heart clean, I am pure from my sin? -PROV. 20:9.

Men who argue their personal sinlessness are exceedingly presumptuous. Such had better take heed lest they fall. Individual salvation never comes from saying "I have made my heart clean"; it is the appropriated gift of God.

PRAYER PETITION:

At the close of each day, I must needs beg forgiveness for sins committed.

SEPTEMBER 2

He first findeth his own brother. -JOHN 1: 41

Evangelism expresses itself in our own family. To be true, it is harder to win members of our own family than any other. The test of our zeal is in finding first those of our own It should be obligatory upon a church member to win one each year to Christ. When we have such a witnessing Church then the Kingdom will have made rapid strides onward.

PRAYER SUGGESTION:

Pray, today, for members of your family.

SEPTEMBER 3

All the ways of a man are clean in his own eyes; but the Lord weigheth the spirit. -PROV. 16:2.

It is interesting to hear men's opinions of

their own merits, The man who in his own eyes is clean is the man of whom we might' well beware. God, alone, is the Judge of the worth of a man. We judge outwardly; -God sees and knows men's motives.

PRAYER PETITION:

Thou readest my motives more accurately than even I am willing to do. Wilt Thou teach me my weaknesses?

SEPTEMBER 4

Knock, and it shall be opened unto you.
- LUKE 11:9.

When we desire to enter a home we knock or ring the bell. 1£ the answer is not immediate and we know the folks are there, we become insistent in our attempt to enter. Persistency in our religious quests is always rewarded with an answer. The blessings of divinity are ours if we knock at its door.

PRAYER PETITION:

When we knock at Thy door, Thou wilt answer. May we never turn a deaf ear to Thy knock at the door of our hearts.

SEPTEMBER 5

He that is slow to anger is better than the
mighty; and he. that ruleth his spirit than he

that taketh a city. -PROV. 16: 3 2.

There is no citadel so difficult to capture as
that of our own heart. We lock our weaknesses
so carefully there, and -treasure them.
Few of us are willing to correct the fault
which we know we have. More difficulties
arise because we will not conquer our tempers,
than for any other one reason. There is
no achievement so worthwhile as the mastery
of self.

PRAYER PETITION:

Make me willing to conquer myself and my
stubborn, human traits. Teach me that to be
Christian, I must strive to be like Thee.

SEPTEMBER 6

*Casting all your care upon Him; for He
careth for you.* -1 PETER 5 :7.

Mortals carry many cares and worries. If
it isn't one thing, it is another. When will we
ever learn that we may cast our cares on
Him? If we have done the best we can,-
that is all we can do. Leave the rest with
God. Lean upon His Spirit to do the things
you, in your strength, cannot do.

PRAYER PETITION:

I know that I am not truly Christian until
I have learned to cast my cares upon Thee.
Thou art anxious to bear my burdens for me.

Few families are there in which some one brother has not yet been found. Pray for him.

SEPTEMBER 7

Let us lay aside ... the sin which doth so easily beset us. -HEB. 12: 1.

Each has a dominant or besetting sin. A man has gone a long ways toward mastering it when he determines what it is. Sin is a weight. It is a liability which a man carries. There is no joy in it; it always demands its, toll. Let us lay it aside. Spiritual joys become yours only as you lay aside material weights.

PRAYER PETITION:

We have prayed that we may have self mastery sufficient to throw aside our favorite sin. Strengthen our purpose, Lord, we pray.

SEPTEMBER 8

If ye forgive ... your Father will forgive you. -MATT. 6:14.

We have studied texts on forgiveness. God in His mercy forgives us our sins. A marvelous thing to feel we are sinless. We have noted that God's blessings involve certain acts upon our part. This is another instance which bears out that thought. "If ye forgive" .... then the Father will forgive you.

PRAYER PETITION:

Forgive us our debts as we forgive our debtors.

SEPTEMBER 9

Jesus wept. -JOHN 11:35.

In the tears of a man you can detect his soul. These two words, constituting the shortest verse in the Bible, teach us Jesus' Sympathy, Humanity, Companionship and Love. At every open grave Jesus shares our sorrow with us. In all of life's problems He expresses the depth of His sympathy.

PRAYER PETITION:

We thank Thee that Thou art a compassionate Friend. Thy tears make us love Thee more.

SEPTEMBER 10

Covet earnestly the best gifts. -1 COR. 12: 31.

Herein is stated: the only legitimate cause for covetousness. Used in one sense the word "covet" is a sin, in another it secures for us life's richest blessings. In one portion of Paul's writings he admonishes us to think on

the best things. Here he suggests we covet
the best things. Many tastes are uncultured.
The best things might be had through little
effort. First things are best gifts.

PRAYER SUGGESTION:

Decide what are the best gifts for yourself.
Pray earnestly for them. It would be well,
too, that we as a church covet and pray for
the best gifts.

SEPTEMBER 11

*Ye know that your labour is not in vain in
the Lord.* -1 COR. 15:58.

I have known men to work at a given task
for years without any perceptible progress. As
workers in God's vineyard, how different the
assurance. Though we may judge our work
a failure, if performed in His strength "your
Iabour is not in vain." A consecrated heart
and a ready mind in harmony with His will
accomplish marvels.

PRAYER PETITION:

Prosper my work, 0 Lord, if it be done
according to Thy will and Thy purpose for me.

SEPTEMBER 12

*One thing I know, that, whereas I was
blind, now I see.* -JOHN 9:25.

When I came to Pontiac as a candidate
three years ago this was the text I used. Upon
the philosophy of this text hinges our entire
Christian faith. Men told the blind man that
Jesus was a sinner. He replied, "Whether he
is a sinner, I know not: one thing I know,
that, whereas I was blind, now I see". Nothing
of religion can be proven to the conviction
of an inquiring doubter. The fact that
it works is its greatest proof.

PRAYER PETITION:

Thou hast opened my eyes and now I can
see the beauties of Thy universe, the goodness
of men and the infinite love of Jesus, my
Saviour.

SEPTEMBER 13

The field is the world. -MATT. 13:38.

These days of rapid transportation are
bringing the world to our very doors. No
nation can longer live alone. Religion is
touching the whole world. Politically, a party
existing for its own nation alone is a dying
force; religiously, that man seeing his own
church or community and not the world is a
dwarfed soul. Christ has failed to touch him.
Our field is the world.

PRAYER PETITION:

We are challenged by the greatness of our

task. May we truly have a world vision. We would extend our services throughout the world by our gifts and our prayers.

SEPTEMBER 14

Thy life is more than meat, and the body is more than raiment. -LUKE 12:23.

It would take some little persuasion to convince many people that this is true. Theoretically, we believe differently; practically, we live as if there were nothing more. "Eat, drink and be merry" for tomorrow we die is the view of many. Such need an eternal vision. Life begun now exists eternally. Moral Ideals are all that destine life for eternal climes.

PRAYER PETITION:

Would that we would give more thought to purity of life and body than we give to our physical needs.

SEPTEMBER 15

Ye also, as lively stones, are built up a spiritual house. -1 PETER 2: 5.

A church is a "spiritual house". Someone once said of church members, "they keep house for God." Members should be "lively stones". Churches exist not for social or recreational purposes but to promulgate spiritual ideals in the hearts of men and women. When the church fails to do this, she will die. However she can never fail because God is her soul.

PRAYER SUGGESTION:

Pray for a keener appreciation of your obligation as a "lively stone" in holding up the structure of our "spiritual house".

SEPTEMBER 16

If, when ye do well and suffer for it, ye take it patiently, this is acceptable with God.
-1 PET. 2:20.

It is difficult, when we have done well, to be criticized. We are so apt to be "up in arms" and rebel at the injustice. O that we might learn to suffer patiently. Our Master when He was reviled, answered not a word. It takes more than patience, it is akin to heroism, yet it is "acceptable to God". That is the reward.

PRAYER PETITION:

Teach me to bear Injustice patiently. May I not seek to take my own part but may I know that Thou art well pleased with my patience.

SEPTEMBER 17

The harvest truly is plenteous but the labourers are few. -MATT. 9:37.

We live in a community where thousands are seeking the influence of a church home. There is no joy akin to that of linking a soul with Christ through the ministry of His church. Each member should feel an individual responsibility in performing this task. Call me today and ask for the names of some upon whom you may call. Laborers are few. We can and should use each member.

PRAYER SUGGESTION:

There are so many opportunities for service in Pontiac, so many people for our church to reach. Perhaps you in your home, offering your prayers, may help to increase the harvest. Pray, then go out to reap.

SEPTEMBER 18

What shall we do, that we might work the works of God? -JOHN 6:28.

This text links itself very nicely with the thought of yesterday. We should pray, read the Bible, call upon those who do not know Him, give of our material possessions, make some sacrifice which hurts. An individual life, thoroughly consecrated, can be used abundantly in His service.

PRAYER SUGGESTION:

If you have called upon strangers or met them elsewhere, if you have made up a prayer

148

list, take these to God in your prayer today.

SEPTEMBER 19

Whosoever shall seek to save his life shall
lose it; and whosoever shall lose his life shall
preserve it. -LUKE 17:33.

This text contains a strange paradox. How
often we find the truth of it carried out in
everyday experience. The man overly careful
regarding his physical well-being is invariably
a sick man. The opposite is likewise true. A
service rendered, forgetful of one's self, enables
us to find depths of personality otherwise
unknown.

PRAYER PETITION:

If I can but lose myself and thoughts of
myself in service rendered in Thy name, Thou
wilt grant unto me the joy of seeing such
influence live in the lives of others.

SEPTEMBER 20

Speak not evil one of another, brethren.
-JAMES 4:11.

I have an ambition. I should like to see a
congregation which agreed before God never
to speak or think evil of one another. The
moment one did he would automatically lose
his identity with that Church. Perhaps such
a church will never be possible this side of

heaven, but if ever such a church becomes an actuality, it will become the greatest force for righteousness in the community where it is located.

PRAYER SUGGESTION:

Can we, unitedly; in our prayer this morning promise our God that if we can speak no good of our brethren, we shall be silent?

SEPTEMBER 21

Seek those things which are above. -COL. 3: 1.

There is an old story of a swan and a crane. The crane contented itself with feasting on snails. The swan advised heavenly things, With indifference the crane replied, "I do not want to go to heaven; I want to feast on snails." Most of us content ourselves with mundane things. Ours should be a passion for things which are above.

PRAYER PETITION:

Grant to me heavenly desires. May I set my affections upon things not of the earth but of above.

SEPTEMBER 22

Then shall we know, if we follow on to. know the Lord. -HOSEA 6: 3.

There is no reason in faith. It is a blind
venture with our hand in God's. Though
groping blindly, we are promised that we shall
know the mystery of things if we follow the
Lord. This text reminds us of 1 Cor. 13: 12;
"Now we see through a glass, darkly; but
then face to face." True knowledge is the
result of a firm faith in God.

PRAYER PETITION:

"Lead Thou me on,-Keep Thou my feet,-
I do not ask to see the distant scene. One step
enough for me."

SEPTEMBER 23

*If ye know these things; happy are ye if ye
do them.* -JOHN 13:17.

Knowledge and action are two different
things. You have often heard it said that some
men are brilliant and others practical. Knowing
something does not give happiness. The
prosecution of knowledge gives happiness. Truth
put into action,-that brings joy.

PRAYER PETITION:

So often we know what to do but never will
so to do. Grant us the happiness of fulfilled
opportunities.

SEPTEMBER 24

*Therefore to him that knoweth to do good,
and doeth It not, to him it is sin.* -JAMES 4:17.
The greatest sin is doing less than our best.
Each should have an object; in falling short
of that goal we commit a sin. Men realize
they should unite with a church. In failing to
do so they sin. Sin is unexecuted knowledge.

PRAYER PETITION:

We would continue to pray as we did
yesterday that we may do the things which we
know to do. May we not be guilty of the sin
of leaving our task undone.

SEPTEMBER 25

*For godliness with contentment is great
gain.* -1 TIM. 6:6.

Most men seek two things in life. The first
of these is personal gain and the second is
contentment. Some feel that a successful life
involves these two things. The text is a sort of
an algebraic equation. It should read: the
relation of gain to godliness gives contentment.

PRAYER PETITION:

Often it is difficult to be content with godly
things. The questionable tempts us, taunts us,
leads us on. Grant us the joy of at last gaining

contentment through godliness.

SEPTEMBER 26

If I take the wings of the morning, and
dwell in the uttermost parts of the sea; even
there shall Thy hand lead me, and Thy right
hand shall hold me. -PS. 139:9-10.

God's love is universal. It knows no geographical
boundaries. It possesses neither time
nor space. It is not confined to earth or
heaven. Wherever we go or whatever we do
His "right hand shall hold me"

PRAYER PETITION:

No where do we go where we shall be apart
from Thee. We thank Thee for Thy ever-
present companionship.

SEPTEMBER 27

Walk worthy of the vocation wherewith ye
are called. -EPH. 4: 1.

Paul in writing this letter to the Ephesians
mentions the word "walk" several times. Here
he challenges them to walk worthy of their
vocation. Dwight L. Moody said of a man,
"That man is a soldier". When asked why, he
replied, "I can tell by the way he walks."
Men judge us every day by the way we walk
as Christians.

PRAYER PETITION:

Permit me not, O Lord, to forget that I
have confessed Thee before men. May they
see in my walk that I am living my profession.

SEPTEMBER 28

*Set a watch, O Lord, before my" mouth;
keep the door of my lips.* -PS. 141:3.

A miniature sentinel might well stand at
one of the corners of our mouths. He, then,
would tell us when to speak and when not to.
Troubles occur not through too little speaking
but because we say too much. God's spirit
can be the "watch". If only we would
check ourselves by asking "Would I say this
if Jesus were present?", then the expressions
of our mouths would be more circumspect.

PRAYER PETITION:

This is truly the prayer of my heart. Seal
my lips that they speak only the words which
Thou puttest into them. May I guard each
word for once it is given out, it may never be
recalled.

SEPTEMBER 29

*That ye ... may be able ... to know the
love of Christ which passeth knowledge.* -EPH.
3:17, 18, 19.

It is difficult to know that which passeth knowledge. A few days ago you read that faith was a blind venture devoid of reason. This text wants us to know that which transcends knowledge. That is where faith comes. in. It is a super-intelligence inspired by the mind of God. The unbreakable love of Christ passeth all human know ledge. It is a challenge to. deepest faith.

PRAYER PETITION:

Increase our knowledge that we may be able to comprehend what is the heighth, and depth and breadth of Thy love for us, 0 Christ.

SEPTEMBER 30

I was afraid, and went and hid thy talent in the earth; lo, there thou hast that is thine.
-MATT. 25:25.

I have always been profoundly sympathetic with this one talented man. Surely there are many such. God exacts more from us than that with which He endows us. He challenges us to grow. A Burbank must perfect Nature's perfect rose. God challenges us to activity. We must return to him a better life than he gave us originally.

PRAYER PETITION:

May any talent which Thou hast invested

in me bring dividends for Thy Kingdom.

OCTOBER 1

I have finished the work which Thou gavest me to do. -JOHN 17:4.

Life is a vineyard staked out by God. Each has his allotted vines to prune and keep. Some have hills to climb; some soil is richer than the other. The consciousness of having completed the work set out for us is life's richest joy. Also, to know that our work, whatever it may be He has given us to do, is life's greatest inspiration.

PRAYER PETITION:

Grant to us the joy of fidelity to our task. Whatever our allotted task may be, insignificant or of great importance, may we at that last day, be able to say "I have finished the work which Thou gavest me to do."

OCTOBER 2

She hath done what she could. -MARK 14:8.

Jesus said of the woman referred to in this text that the deed should be a memorial unto her. False excuses characterize most of our lives. Few of us do nearly what we could. When Jesus found one who did what she could, it is no small wonder that He sought to memorialize her. Let us strive, this month, to do our best.

PRAYER PETITION:

We thank Thee that Thou dost not expect us to do more than we are able. Thou dost commend when we do what we can.

OCTOBER 3

Nor trust in uncertain riches, but in the living God, who giveth us richly all things to enjoy. -1 TIM. 6:17.

If we could all be given a wish most of us would desire material things. Money can buy almost any thing. In spite of this instinctive desire, each of us has seen the uncertainty of riches. Nothing material endures. The Living God endures through all generations and all that we need, He supplies. All that is needful for our joy, He gives.

PRAYER PETITION:

It is difficult for us to distinguish between uncertain riches and those which Thou giveth. Grant to us a contentment in the real riches of life.

OCTOBER 4

Serve Him with a perfect heart, and with a willing mind. -1 CHRON. 28:9.

Christian service must be rendered willingly and from the heart. Often you find men in church work who serve from a sense of horrid duty. Such service does not gladden the heart of God. Only the spontaneous act from a happy mind receives a blessing from the Divine.

PRAYER PETITION:

Take from our hearts the reluctant spirit with which we so often enter into our work for Thee and Thy Church. Make us to love Thy service.

OCTOBER 5

Them that were entering in, ye hindered.
-LUKE 11:52.

In this entire chapter Jesus preaches with great power. He minces no words. The text is used against the lawyers. How readily it applies to all of us. Think of the many whom we have hindered in the Christian life. Each of us has someone who, unknown to us, looks to us as his example. Have we hindered him from making the progress he ought?

PRAYER PETITION:

Ask yourself the question frankly, "Am I hindering anyone from entering the Church?" Then go to your knees and pray that if so, the reasons for such objections may be erased from your life.

OCTOBER 6

*Let Him do to me as seemeth good unto
Him.* -2 SAM. 15:26.

Most of us go through life with a chip on
our shoulder. We are ever in an attitude of
self-defense, eager to rise in our own behalf.
The king gives Zadok some sound advice;
"Throw yourself upon His mercy and let Him
do what seems best to Him." The vindicative
soul is always in trouble. The one who throws
himself open to disadvantage never is taken
advantage of.

PRAYER PETITION:

I have absolute confidence in Thy mercy
and Thy justice. What is best for me, Thou
knowest. Use me as Thou dost see fit.

OCTOBER 7

*In lowliness of mind let each esteem. other
better than themselves.* -PHIL 2:3.

Much affectation is possible in applying this
text. When done in sincerity, nothing so
clearly reveals true character. A strong man
is never conscious of his strength. No one
will be more astounded than he if told of his
ability. Jealousies are not merely human; they
are heathenish. No man is really great who is

159

jealous of another. Let us "esteem other better than ourselves."

PRAYER SUGGESTION:

Is there 'some one of whom you are exceedingly jealous? Admit it to yourself and to God. Your confession may be the means of ridding your heart of such pettiness.

OCTOBER 8

Trust in the Lord, and do good; so shall thou dwell in the land, and verily thou shall be fed. -PS. 37:3.

This text holds significant values in proper relationship to expected results. In life, men seek to be fed; they desire success and yet fail to realize that these things come only by trusting in God and doing good. The proper emphasis of life is lost.

PRAYER PETITION:

Many things which we do in Thy name, Father, we do because we feel we must, not because we would do good. Grant us the desire to be of real service.

OCTOBER 9

Keep thy foot when thou goest to the house of God. -ECC. 5:1.

Many temptations come to us on a Sabbath day, Golf sticks cry out to be exercised; fish challenge us to catch them; the fields and meadows invite us to lounge. We must needs keep our feet and our heads as well in these days of varied attractions. The Church is made up of individuals and its strength is no greater than the weakest member.

PRAYER PETITION:

I would walk circumspectively as I enter Thy house, 0 Father. There may be little feet which shall tread in my footsteps. May I take the straight path which leads to Thee.

OCTOBER 10

The shadow of a great rock in a weary land. -ISA. 32:2.

Picture a desert, devoid of trees or water. A great rock is in the distance. Approaching it, we rest in its shade and feel the coolness of its breath upon our cheek. In a world of screaming activity, God is a rock to a weary land.

PRAYER PETITION:

"On Christ, the Solid Rock, I stand;
All other ground is sinking sand."

OCTOBER 11

There are diversities of operations, but it is the same God which worketh all in all. -1 COR. 12:6.

Life has many activities. The field of industry throbs with activity. Business becomes increasingly prosperous. Minds are shrewder. Racial differences are extenuated by the rise of color. No Law or Mind seems to be linking all these activities into a united purpose. Ah! but the words of the text offer a solution. Read the text again and see if these problems are not somewhat alleviated

PRAYER PETITION:

Guard me lest I judge another's life by my standards. Help me to remember that he worships Thee, the One God, but his approach to Thee may be different.

OCTOBER 12

Thine own friend, and thy father's friend, forsake not. -PROV. 27:10.

Friendship is woven out of the threads of sympathy, understanding, respect and mutual interest. There are many acquaintanceships, but few friendships. Everyone should have one friend. Friendship should be an eternal thing surviving a generation. The friend of one's father should be committed to his son.

I would that I might appreciate the
sanctity of friendship. God grant that I may
never sever friendships by any deed or mine.

OCTOBER 13

Let us rise up and build. -NEH. 2:18.

Christians should be challenged by this text
to rise up and build the eternal structure of
character. Nations should be builded upon
principles of idealism. Churches should build
for world service. Sinners should build saved
souls. Those living merely for this life should
build eternal mansions. Rise up! Build!

PRAYER SUGGESTION:

Is our church building those things which
shall live eternally in the lives of those who
are a part of her structure? Pray that she
may truly rise up and build.

OCTOBER 14

Where hast thou gleaned today? -RUTH 2:19.

Naomi asked this question of Ruth. She
did so in the hope that Providence was working
His wonders to perform. Like all good
stories it turned out that way. Boaz wooed
and won her, and their child, abed, was a link
in the genealogy of Jesus. Ruth found happiness

because she did her allotted task with a
faith in God.

PRAYER SUGGESTION:

What have you gleaned today? Pray that
no single day may pass in which you have not
entered into God's field to serve as a gleaner
there.

OCTOBER 15

*The fool hath said in his heart, There is no
God.* -PSALM 53: 1.

Some learned minds look askance at the
believing soul. Seemingly it is a sign of great
intellect to be able to deny the reality of God.
To destroy a faith requires no brains; to build
a faith involves tremenduous strength. With
those who deny I have no argument. I permit
the Psalmist to say his word, "The fool . . .
said there is no God."

PRAYER PETITION:

I would daily affirm my belief in Thee, my
God. Forbid that I ever be so foolish as to in
any way deny Thee.

OCTOBER 16

*Say not thou, what is the cause that the
former days were better than these?* -Ecc.7:10.

One would hardly suppose that a text of such modern significance could be found in the Scriptures. Those who hold that former days were better than these had better meditate upon this text. Why should former days be better? God has not left His creation alone. To maintain its failure would be to belittle God.

PRAYER PETITION:

Thou art in Thy heavens, all must be well with the world.

OCTOBER 17

I have set thee for a tower and a fortress among my people. -JER. 6:27.

Jeremiah is charged by God to be "a tower and a fortress" among his people. To be located in a tower enables one to see great distances and the approach of the enemy. A fortress affords protection. As Christians we should be a tower set up and seen of people; a fortress of peace by which disturbed souls might find rest.

PRAYER SUGGESTION:

God has set us apart to protect His cause against those who seek to destroy His work. Are we doing so? Pray, that never by any act of ours shall the enemies of Christianity be enabled to enter our stronghold.

OCTOBER 18

*Perplexed, but not in despair; ... cast
down, but not destroyed. -2 COR. 4:8, 9.*

It will do our souls much good to memorize
this text. There will come many an opportunity
to use it. How human it sounds! Paul
reveals his determination and persistence. Life
is perplexing, but not despairing. It casts us
down, but can't destroy us. Let us look up to
Him who guides and protects.

PRAYER PETITION:

Thou hast promised that Thou wilt never
permit us to bear more than we are able. We
are thankful for the note of trust and security
which Thy promises sound.

OCTOBER 19

*Every tree is known by its own fruit. -LUKE
6:44.*

Look at a fruit and you can always tell the
species of the tree. The quality of the fruit
invariably reflects upon the strength of the
tree. Our sustenance, as Christians, should
come from Christ, our Tree. If the fruit is
spotty or withered, only one is judged,-the
Christ. Only as we keep ourselves attached
to Him can the spots be removed.

PRAYER PETITION:

What fruit am I bearing, O Tree of Life?
Permit that I shall so take vitality from the
Tree that I shall be a fruit-bearing branch.
In good fruit may I make known my Christ.

OCTOBER 20

He that loveth not his brother whom he
hath seen, how can he love God whom he hath
not seen? -1 JOHN 4:20.

There is nothing in Scripture more emphatic
than this. Love toward our fellowmen
is obligatory if we profess love for God. One
is dependent upon the other. The surest proof
of lack of love toward God is hatred toward
our fellowmen. There are no two ways about
it. You can't quibble. These are the facts.
Read the text again.

PRAYER SUGGESTION:

We cannot pray too often for love in our
hearts toward our fellowmen. This is the
best proof of our love for God. Pray for such
an all-enhancing love.

OCTOBER 21

As having nothing, and yet possessing all
things. -2 COR. 6:10.

Paul also writes "all is yours." Poverty is
simply a state of mind. There is always food
and clothes to be had if only one exerts some

initiative. A covetous eye causes discontentment. Looking at the universe with its streams and flowers, cities with their museums and books, parks and beauty spots, enables one to know that "all is yours." The poor man receives as many dividends from these as the rich. Then, too, "all things" are found in Christ. Here is the proof of a man's wealth.

PRAYER SUGGESTION:

Review for yourselves the things which you have. Are they not the best things of life, the essential things? Thank God for them.

OCTOBER 22

That we may lead a quiet and peaceable life. . ... -1 TIM. 2:2.

Hurrying, worrying, scampering aimlessly- this depicts modern 'life. Our nerves are torn to shreds; we hasten nowhere to a shifting object. Some day this goalless race of human kind will have to stop. Progress continues too rapidly for humanity to enjoy it. The text is a solution. Walking humbly before God gives us quiet and peace. Even in a restless age these can satisfy.

PRAYER PETITION:

Grant to us contentment in the quiet, happy, peaceable things of life. We do not pray that we shall cease to be vitally alive, but that we shall find in Thee and in lasting realities, quiet and peace.

OCTOBER 23

Be ye therefore perfect, even as your Father which is in heaven is perfect. -MATT. 5:48.

This is a challenge which we in our sins cannot thoroughly comprehend. Only our Christ was perfect; how can we equal or supersede His moral attainment. Have you read the text? To assume the possibility of attaining the suggestion savors of blasphemy. But this is our task. What progress have you made in the last several years?

PRAYER PETITION:

We do pray that we may begin to approach unto Thy perfectness. Thou hast given Thyself as our Example. We would will to strive to be like Thee.

OCTOBER 24

Bear ye one another's burdens, and so fulfill the law of Christ. -GAL. 6:2.

Human experience demands mutual burden-bearing. We fulfill the law of Christ as we do this. Men may take advantage of you but this does not relieve you of your responsibility. One may seek you in the midst of a busy day. Your inclination is to be indifferent and cold.

Perhaps God sent this person to you. You should share his burden.

PRAYER SUGGESTION:

Are you too busy bearing your own burdens to be interested in those of another? Carry the burdens of another today and lay them at the feet of our Willing Burden Bearer. He will aid you both.

OCTOBER 25

I will arise and go to my Father. -LUKE 15:18.

When we are convicted of our sin there is only one thing to do,-arise and go to our Father. The Prodigal had tired of sin. In all its glamor, sin was no longer as inviting as his father's home. So he returned! Is it not interesting to note that the Father comes more than half way to receive us if only we make the decision to "arise and go"?

PRAYER SUGGESTION:

Arise today and go to your Heavenly Father. Take your sins and your discouragements, your perplexities, your joys and your sorrows. He will receive you into His all-embracing arms.

OCTOBER 26

Finally, my brethren, be strong in the Lord,
and in the power of His might. -EPH. 6:10.

There could be no greater conclusion to a
sermon than this. The poem by Maltbie B.
Babcock should be read in connection with
this text. It is entitled "Be Strong."
"Be strong!
We are not here to play,-to dream, to drift.
We have hard work to do, a load to lift."
Let us as Christians be Strong and Powerful
through His might.

PRAYER PETITION:

Strengthen Thou us with Power from Thy
mighty self. We need to be strong to face
life bravely; and "If there be some weaker one,
give me strength to help him on."

OCTOBER 27

Why stand ye here all the day idle? -MATT.
20:6.

There is work for everyone in the Kingdom.
No one can stand around offering the excuse.
"Because no man hath hired us." We are eternally
in the employ of our Master. The tasks
are here, we must find them. Those pastimes
are dangerous which produce idleness. Only
those things which inspire us to activity arc
good. An acquitted obligation is our daily

responsibility.

PRAYER PETITION:

I bow in shame before Thee, O Christ, I
have stood idly by, all the. day, while others
served Thee. Now I come to Thee, asking a
task to perform.

OCTOBER 28

This is the day which the Lord hath made:
we will rejoice and be glad in it. -Ps. 118:24.

God has made every day. Each is significant.
The Sabbath is a physiological necessity. To
be well physically men must change their
occupation one day out of seven. There is no
rest akin to communion with Him in God's
house. Sunday newspapers, an afternoon nap
and a round of golf are not nearly the equal
in restorative ability of one sincere hour spent
in the house of God.

PRAYER SUGGESTION:

Pray today for God's blessing to be upon
your Church this day. Pray for her services,
her minister and the message which shall be
brought.

OCTOBER 29

And when he saw a fig tree in the way, he
came to it, and found nothing thereon, but

leaves only. -MATT. 21:19.

This fig tree is symbolical of many lives. Too many of us have the appearance of a fruitful Christian life, whereas upon closer scrutiny "nothing but leaves" is found. There is no greater tragedy. An affected life is a hell. A conscious hypocrite is dead already. Merely an outward profession produces a charred soul.

PRAYER PETITION:

O God, do others see in my life nothing but leaves? Thou 'canst read my motives. Thou knowest whether I would bear fruit or whether I am but a fruitless affectation.

OCTOBER 30

He that is faithful in that which is least is faithful also in much. -LUKE 16:10.

A successful man is not the one who does only the big things. He is marvelously efficient at details. True culture sees not only the fastidious but the humble as well. Loyalty to little things makes us ruler over great responsibilities. Faithfulness to one's Church produces the highest type of citizenship in the secular affairs of life.

PRAYER PETITION:

Too often we feel that only in big things can we prove our faithfulness to our task and to

Thee. Grant that I may understand that as I perform the little services, am I fit for the grander tasks.

OCTOBER 31

I am Alpha and Omega. -REV. 22:13.

These Greek words are the first and last letters in the Greek alphabet. Thus, they mean the first and the last. In Genesis 1: 1 we read, "In the beginning God...." At the creation of the universe and of man, we find God. At the end of life when our fading consciousness sees none other-there is God.

PRAYER PETITION:

It is sweet to know that Thou hadst prepared a place for us before we came into this world and in that other land, Thou hast a place for us there.

NOVEMBER 1

Who hath despised the day of small things? -ZECH. 4:10.

There are many dangers in an age like this. Automobile parts, which formerly took days to manufacture, are now constructed in a few seconds. The big things are done with marked efficiency. The danger is that we will neglect the "small things." Churches and Religion must not be forgotten because tremendous

opportunities knock at other doors. The
day of Judgment will come. A moron race will
confront us if we despise "the day of small
things."

PRAYER PETITION:

Again we ask Thee to teach us the grandeur
of little tasks. It takes a little child to make
a man; it took a Babe in the manger to give
us Jesus. May we never despise little things.

NOVEMBER 2

*Enlarge the place of thy tent ...spare
not, lengthen thy cords, and strengthen. thy
stakes.* -ISA. 54:2.

Yesterday I sought to get you to minimize
your efforts; this text is a challenge to growth.
Our minds should be enlarged. Nine billion
brain cells afford much opportunity for mental
growth. Social relationships should be developed.
Growth is indispensable; but-
"strengthen thy stakes." Be sure to hold fast
to life's eternal moorings.

PRAYER SUGGESTION:

Too often we confine our prayers to our
immediate circle, our family, our friends, our
Church. Today enlarge your tent. Include
your nation, her officials, other nations, even
unto the uttermost parts of the world.

NOVEMBER 3

Consider the lilies of the field, how they grow. -MATT. 6:28.

Every man worries about making a living. He 'is not selfish, desiring things only for himself; he wants to assure the future of his family. On the face of it, nothing is more commendable; investigated more closely-nothing as ridiculous. Our times are in God's hands. Carefulness on our part to provide all the details of life does not remove God from the universe. Lilies make no preparation for the future and yet God enables them to grow and prosper.

PRAYER PETITION:

Daily we prove our lack of faith. by our anxieties. May I today in all things remember that even the hairs of my head are numbered; that not even a sparrow falls but Thou dost care. Surely then, Lord God, Thou wilt care for me.

NOVEMBER 4

Remember ye not the former things, neither consider the things of old. -ISA. 43: 18.

Many years ago, in the early hours of the morning, I tossed sleeplessly in a little cabin on the Baltic Sea. The storm without was reflected in my soul. My conscience was acutely sensitive. The sins of my youth faced me. My mother, lying in an adjacent room, comforted- me with the suggestion that God had forgiven me and that I should go to sleep. "Remember ye not the former things, neither consider the things of God."

PRAYER PETITION:

I pray for an onward and upward look, O Lord, onward to a more perfect life hid in Thee, upward into Thy very presence. May I never glance back, lest I, too, become "a pillar of salt."

NOVEMBER 5

Be strong, and of good courage, dread not, nor·be dismayed. -1 CHRON. 22:13.

This text challenges us to be Strong, Courageous, Fearless. Many problems may confront us today. Temptation's siren-like voice may plead with us to do the wrong. We can be the things the text suggests if "we live, move and have our being in God."

PRAYER PETITION:

It is so difficult to be strong and courageous. Thou knowest, Father, the perplexities that arise, the anxieties that harass, the temptations which flaunt their fascinations before us. Uphold Thou us, in our determination that we face the fight, even the unseen enemies, bravely.

NOVEMBER 6

My times are in Thy hand. -PS. 31:15 .

Time is eternal. We try to confine it into
three score years and ten, but it never began
and it never ends. The text reads, "my times
are in Thy hand." Whether we live or die, we
are God's. This differs from Fatalism in that
God is in it. There is no greater comfort
in life than the consciousness that "my times
are in Thy hand."

PRAYER PETITION:

There would be no reason for life, indeed it
would be a hideous farce, if we had not the
assurance of Thy protecting arms about us.
Even in that last day, we but go to sleep in
the arms of our King.

NOVEMBER 7

Every purpose of the Lord shall be performed.
-JER. 51:29.

This universe is dominated by Purpose. Will
permeates its every law. Nothing happens
which is not the expression of Purpose. Though
to us an accident, the "Purpose of the Lord"
takes the event and harmoniously adjusts it to
His will. Nothing occurs which has not the
stamp of God upon it. Finite eyes cannot see
this. Only faith can believe.
PRAYER PETITION:

May I never be so presumptuous as to feel
that I can work out my own purposes for my
life. I am Thine, not my own, and Thy purpose
for me shall be performed.

NOVEMBER 8

The kingdom of God is within you. -LUKE
17:21.

There are many theories regarding the Kingdom.
Some hold that the world is getting
worse, and when it is bad enough, Christ will
come and establish His Kingdom. Others
maintain it is getting better and when good
enough Christ will come, and establish Himself.
Some others profess a faith in eternal
principles here and now culminating in the
Kingdom. The text is sufficient for now;
it takes care of tomorrow if "the Kingdom
of God is within you."

PRAYER SUGGESTION:

We pray and rightly so, for the universal
Kingdom of God. When we do so we pray
that His Kingdom may come in the heart of
each individual. Shall we pray together today,
"Thy kingdom come, thy will be done,
On earth as it is in Heaven."

NOVEMBER 9

Shall a man make gods unto himself? -JER.
16:20.

"Thou shalt have no other gods before me."
So reads the first Commandment. A god is he
whom we worship above everything else. He
must be personal. Some men make gods of
their business. Social activities are gods to
some women. A god is that something which
holds precedence over the Living God.
Catalogue the number of gods dominating your
life.

PRAYER SUGGESTION:

What are your gods? Is it your home, your
child, your business, your money, your fame?
Turn in worship to the One true God. As
you meet Him more intimately in prayer, you
will grow to know Him better and love Him
more. Pray.

NOVEMBER 10

As the clay is in the potter's hand, so are ye
in mine hand. -JER. 18:6.

He who disbelieves this text will no doubt
harp upon the significance of his own personal
will. We are not machines, but free moral
agents.' This is true, but if God is all in all,
and He made our wills, surely He has power to
dominate them. I like to think of our lives
as "clay in the potter's hand." He moulds
us; He forms us into what we shall become.

PRAYER PETITION:

"God loves to work III clay, not marble-
let Him find,
When He would mould thine heart, material
to His mind."
So a Potter Divine, make me as pleasing
clay in Thy hand."

NOVEMBER 11

Be ye kind one to another. -EPH. 4:32.

Henry Drummond in "The Greatest Thing
in the World" analyzed love through a Prism.
As light separates into different colors, so love
breaks up into different elements. We can do
the same thing with kindness. Broken into
component parts we find that it embraces
Sympathy, Tenderness, Goodness, Humaness
and Benevolence. In Kindness we express all
these qualities.

PRAYER SUGGESTION:

Pray that we may come to an appreciation
of the God that each of us longs for kindness;
that, as we would receive, so may we give out.

NOVEMBER 12

*Can any hide himself in secret places that I
shall not see him?* -JER. 23 :24.

Adam tried to hide himself from God, knowing
that he had sinned. Men always try to
do this. There is no place we can go where

God does not see us. Every act of man is
disclosed to God. We can never win at "hide-
and-seek" with God.

PRAYER SUGGESTION:

Are you hiding yourself away from God?
You are but fooling yourself for He sees you
all the while. Come out into the open and deal
with Him fairly. Go to Him now and He
will welcome you. He will forgive even your
secret sins and wipe them out, if you confess.

NOVEMBER 13

Be not conformed to this world; but be ye
transformed by the renewing of your mind.
-ROM. 12: 2.

Man possesses an innate twist. The kinks
can be disentangled in only one way. No mind
is sane which is not transformed. No life is
balanced which is not reborn. Conformity to
a world devoid of God is worse than heathenism.
A mind renewed by God is all that can
save humanity from its innate perversities.

PRAYER PETITION:

Cleanse Thou my mind. Rid it of the filth
of the world. Renew it with the things which
are lovely, which are true, which are honest,
which are of good report. May I think only
upon these things.

NOVEMBER 14

*Surely the Lord is in this place; and I knew
it not.* -GEN. 28:16.

This is the confession of Jacob. A Bethel
experience should come to every life. Wherever
we lay our head, "the Lord is in this
place." In our Church worship this is true.
Pause for a moment. Do you realize that at
this very moment, wherever you are, God is
with you? Most of us do not fully realize it.
a for a faith to see and know!

PRAYER SUGGESTION:

Pray that, today, you may know that wherever
you go, God goes with you. Pray that
you may go nowhere in which you would be
ashamed to be seen by Christ or to have Christ
seen by others.

NOVEMBER 15

*Man's goings are of the Lord; how can a
man then understand his own way?* –PROV.
20:24.

I am always conscious of men smiling at my
ignorance, when in my own words I state the
substance of this text. My children can be
lost in the big city; but I can help them find
their way. So it is with man. God is his
Father and he can "understand his own way"
only through His guidance.

PRAYER PETITION:

I seek in vain to plan my life. I cannot, a
Lord, for my times are in Thy hand. Thou
dost govern my going out and my coming in.
I thank Thee that my goings are Thine, else I
should lead myself so far astray.

NOVEMBER 16

Is it nothing to you, all ye that pass by?
-LAM. 1:12.

The stream of life flows on. Many of us are
interested only in our own little group. Problems
of gigantic import are being coped with
by consecrated minds. The heathen call
for the gospel. The sick cry for succor. "Is
it nothing to you." A Christian knows life's
problems and does all he can to solve them.

PRAYER PETITION:

I pray for deeper interest in all whom I see
about me. May I be deeply concerned with the
progress of the Church and Thy cause universal.
0 that it may mean more to me! May
I never pass by on the other side, but may I
pause, may I even hinder my progress if I
find a service to be rendered.

NOVEMBER 17

. . .. Mary, which also sat at Jesus' feet,
and heard his word. -LUKE 10:39.

Martha and Mary depict two types of mortals.
Each ran to extremes. "Martha was
cumbered about much serving." She is the
type of woman who becomes discouraged with
her Church because the only knowledge she has
of it is by way of the kitchen. Mary is the
type who is interested only in the spiritual.
Jesus, of course, preferred that type. A
combination of the spiritual and the service
elements makes an ideal type for this day and age.

PRAYER SUGGESTION:

Shall we not, as did Mary, sit quietly at
Jesus' feet this morning, and permit Him to
speak to us. He can unfold such glorious vistas
before us, if we have ears to hear and eyes
to see.

NOVEMBER 18

Why are ye so fearful? How is it that ye
have no faith? -MARK 4:40.

Social life carries with it many problems,
Many things about its complexities engender
fear. "The world is going to the dogs," some
say. How can they? Only the faithless speak
in such terms. God created this world and
still sustains it.

PRAYER PETITION:

Do we yet continue to disclose our lack of
faith? Why, 0 God, do we fear? It must

needs be the constant cry of our hearts that
Thou wilt reveal, to us how to live fearlessly,
how to have more trust and faith in Thee.
Hear our Cry!

NOVEMBER 19

Keep yourselves in the love of God. -JUDE
21.

To do this requires effort. The word "keep"
suggests this. Mortals do not do this instinctively.
We must fight for our religious experience
each day. The world with its responsibilities
crowds in and takes all our time. Well
might we add, "Fight to keep yourselves in the
love of God."

PRAYER PETITION:

Thou are always ready to bestow Thy love
upon us if we but keep ourselves worthy. May
we today strive to keep ourselves in Thy love.

NOVEMBER 20

Nothing shall be impossible unto you. -MATT.
17:20.

This promise is dependent upon our faith.
Of all weeds, a mustard weed is the most despised.
Yet Jesus said, "If ye have faith as a
grain of mustard seed this mountain
shall remove." There is no limiting
your physical or mental abilities, if your

faith is sufficient.

PRAYER PETITION:

May I enter into each task which faces me in
the spirit of the text of today. I can accomplish
all things through Christ, which strengtheneth
me.

NOVEMBER 21

*Whatsoever is brought upon thee, take
cheerfully.* -ECCLESIASTICUS 2 :4.

Scowls accomplish no good. Bitter denunciation
of the afflictions of life never made any
one well. Unhappiness because of the death
of a loved one never brought him back. The
text is difficult to practice, but it will bring
joy.

PRAYER PETITION:

Breathe something of Thy joy into my life,
Lord, that I may see the good in all things.
May I face whatever is brought upon me,
cheerfully.

NOVEMBER 22

*Whatsoever thy hand findeth to do, do it
with thy might.* -ECCL. 9:10.

Few of us do the best we can. A fifty percent
average catches most of us. To make

people think we do better than this we build
a structure of alibis. This text should apply
especially to church members. We find time
to do secular work with all our might,-but
our church reseponsibility is squeezed in hurriedly,
the last moment. Let us put first things
first.

PRAYER PETITION:

So often, Lord, I put aside tasks because I
would wait for a more convenient season, Perhaps,
I am tired and' would not be disturbed.
o God, whatever must be done, may I do it,
gladly and with all my might.

NOVEMBER 23

*For what thanks can we render to God
Again...? -1 THESS. 3 :9.*

Thanksgiving Day is less than a week off.
I have chosen texts appropriate for the season
to consider from now until them. Special days
become a habit. Words become mere repetitions.
How can we render thanks in a new
and fresh way?

PRAYER SUGGESTION:

Through these days preceding Thanksgiving,
shall we not truly render thanks unto God for
His goodness.

NOVEMBER 24

*For all things are for your sakes, that the
abundant grace might through the thanksgiving of many redound to the glory of God.
-II COR. 4: 1 5.*

We can be thankful that all things in life are
"for your sakes." As we give thanks, especially
for the grace or favor of God, so shall
God be glorified. Men shall praise God through
your thankfulness.

PRAYER PETITION:

For Thy grace bestowed upon our lives, we
thank Thee. May we glorify Thee in our con-
duct.

NOVEMBER 25

*Enter into His gates with thanksgiving, and
into his courts with praise, be thankful. unto
Him and bless His name. -PS. 100:4.*

As you go to church this morning, do so
cheerfully. Church going often becomes such
a habit that we go in a machine-like manner.
Carry a smile in your heart and express it
upon your lips. Walk with a lighter step-
be courteously kind to all whom you meet. As
I sit in the pulpit I shall expect to see upturned
toward me, the most cheerful and thankful
congregation I have ever seen. "Let's do this
today.

PRAYER SUGGESTION:

This Sabbath Day, thank Him for your
church; thank Him that you live in a Christian
land, in which the doors of the Church are
open wide to all who will enter.

NOVEMBER 26

*Both riches and honour come of thee, and
thou reignest over all; and in "thine hand is
power and might; and in thine hand it is to
make great, and to give strength unto all.*
-I CHRON. 29:12.

We have a perfect right to be thankful for
all the things mentioned in this text. "Riches"
are loaned us of God. Let us be sure that we
recognize that they are "loaned" us as his
stewards. Honour or renown is not the result
of our personal effort;-God saw fit to
reward us. Thank Him! All we are or hope
to become, God has made possible. Surely
our status, whatever it may be, gives us
occasion to be thankful.

PRAYER SUGGESTION:

You have health, you have strength, you
have the needful things of life. Thank God
for them.

NOVEMBER 27

By him therefore let us offer the sacrifice of

190

praise to God continually, that is, the fruit
of our lips giving thanks to his name. -HEB.
13: 15.

Thanksgiving should be a continual thing.
Not only should it be in our hearts but
expressed by our lips. Such expression is holy;
it is a "sacrifice" to God. The occasion for
greatest thankfulness is for God the Father
Almighty.

PRAYER SUGGESTION:

Often we feel gratitude which we never express. Those who do for us, and God, too,
welcome "the fruit of our lips giving thanks"
and praise.

NOVEMBER 28

We give Thee thanks, O Lord God Almighty,
which art, and wast, and art to come,
because Thou hast taken to Thee Thy great
power and hast reigned. -REV. 11: 17.

We should be thankful for the everlastingness
of God-"which art, and wast, and art to
come." If the world were in the hands of
Satan then we would have cause for alarm.
We can be thankful that Power is God's and
that He reigns supreme over the universe.

PRAYER PETITION:

We thank Thee, for the everlastingness of

Thyself. In this thought, have we the assurance of immortality for we know that as Thou hast given us life, when that mortal life is at an end, Thou wilt take us to Thyself who "art to come."

NOVEMBER 29

O give thanks unto the Lord; for he is good; for His mercy endureth forever. -PS. 118:29.

It is well for you to read this entire chapter. The first two clauses of this text are found at least six times in the Old Testament. Meet as a family this morning. If you are away visiting friends, or friends are at your home, give the day a hallowed meaning by enumerating the things for which you are thankful. Offer them in sincerity, not as statements expected of you.

PRAYER SUGGESTION:

Be thankful. Give God praise.

NOVEMBER 30

When I awake, I am still with Thee. -PS. 139:18.

God is an Abiding Companion. He never leaves us. His spirit, like the fragrance of a precious flower, is ever at our side. We read, somewhere, that though we go into the very pits of hell-He is there. In the morning,

when our eyes first open, what a sweet
consciousness that, "I am still with Thee."

PRAYER PETITION:

Whether we awaken here, or there, I am still
with Thee. I lie down to sleep in peace, knowing
that Thou watchest beside me.

DECEMBER 1

*When I sit in darkness, the Lord shall be a
light unto me.* -MICAH 7:8.

There are many attractive features about our
evening services. One of them is the prayer
period. All the lights in the auditorium are
extinguished and a huge search light from the
outside is turned on a beautiful window directly
behind me. The window depicts Christ
at the home in Emmaus. While I pray the
congregation sits in darkness, looking; if they
care to, at the light of the Lord in the darkness.
The analogy is obvious.

PRAYER PETITION:

I am in darkness unless Thou lighten my
way. Thy presence sends out glowing rays
into every corner of my life.

DECEMBER 2

*Blessed are the pure in heart; for they shall
see God.* -MATT. 5:8.

Evil cannot see purity. World engrossed souls cannot comprehend the things born of spiritualities. Only the pure in heart can see God. These have the favor of God.

PRAYER PETITION:

We pray so often that we may be pure in heart, yet we permit ourselves to be tainted again with lewd reading, with contact with the filth of the world, with unclean thoughts. Purify Thou me that I may see Thee.

DECEMBER 3

But be ye doers of the word, and not bearers only, deceiving your own selves. -JAMES 1 :22.

It always seems strange to me that a score of years of Christian nurture do not make a greater impression upon a life. You and I know hundreds of people who have been in regular attendance at church services for scores of years and yet, seemingly, the treatment has not accomplished good. One of these things is possible: either the patient is immune, the medicine has no value, or the physician is a quack. Maybe the reason is, as the scripture suggests, that such are hearers only, and not "doers of the word."

PRAYER SUGGESTION:
Ask yourselves whether we have heard and read the Word through these months without any attempt to be doers. Our prayer must be

that we shall be doers.

DECEMBER 4

In your patience possess ye your souls. -LUKE
21: 19.

Impatience characterizes most of us. All
that we do. is done in a hurry. Our rapidly
moving civilization is largely responsible for
this. People of depth are patient folks. The
strong character can be measured by his patience.
The text, seemingly, is modernly worded.
It is a gem of philosophical truth.

PRAYER PETITION:

Teach me patience-patience in. the midst
of tribulation, patience under criticism, patience
when harrassed by a multiplicity of tasks.
In patience, Father, possess, I my soul.

DECEMBER 5

*Whatsoever a man soweth, that shall be also
reap.* -GAL. 6:7.

Here we have a biological truth brought into
the realm of morals. Carelessness begets carelessness;
evil thoughts can but express themselves
in a sinful life. Sow a thought and you
reap a habit. Nature's laws are inviolable;
moral laws are as exacting as Nature's.

PRAYER PETITION:

What, O God, am I sowing? What shall I
reap? Help me that I stop now, at this moment,
to look over the field of my life. Tear
out the weeds and the tares, and leave but
fruitful grain.

DECEMBER 6

He giveth power to the faint; and to them
that have no might He increaseth strength.
-ISA. 40:29.

In the early morning hours, our bodies refreshed
from a night's rest; love in the home
inspiring us for the activities of the day, we
little feel the significance of this text. But
when the day's problems press in, when we
grow faint from weariness, then we need be
stimulated. There is no normal refreshment
of strength that does not touch the spirit. He
gives Power and Strength.

PRAYER SUGGESTION:

"Art thou weary, art thou languid, art thou
sore distressed? "Come to me," saith One,
"and coming, be at rest."

DECEMBER 7

Seekest thou great things for thyself? Seek
them not. -JER. 45: 5.

We are reminded of Jesus' suggestion that
he who would find his life shall lose it. Popularity

cannot be sought, it is a reward of merit.
Wealth cannot be bought, it is the return of
service. Material things cannot be sought and
attained. Self greatness is not the result of our
own conscious effort, it is the estimation of
another of our effort. The strong character
is not conscious of his power.

PRAYER PETITION:

Each of us seek things selfishly for us. We
have ambitions which we seek to realize, we
have desires to satisfy, rich things which we
want to possess. Make Thou us unselfish.

DECEMBER 8

*Blessed are the peacemakers; for they shall be
called the children of God.* -MATT. 5 :6:

I have often told of a man who carried an oil
can with him everywhere he went. When a
door creaked, out came the can and a drop was
administered to the hinge. Most folks are not
like the Oil Can Man. Humans are morbidly
interested in discord and strife. No greater
work can be done by a Christian than to go
through life an honest, positive, peacemaker.
Carrying water on both shoulders is not being
a peacemaker. Harmony in one's own heart is
the greatest assurance of peace.

PRAYER SUGGESTION:

We each need to be peacemakers. Many of

us add untrue notes to discordancies already existing. Pray today that we may be peace-makers, else we are not true children of God.

DECEMBER 9

The eternal God is thy refuge, and underneath are the everlasting arms. -DEUT. 33 :27.

I have no idea what might have been in the writer's mind when he wrote this text but it presents a picture to my mind. Picture your-self on a mountain. A storm comes up hurriedly. The canyon below yawns for you with outstretched arms. Beneath an overhanging rock, you are given refuge and underneath, holding you lest you slip, is your guide. God, our Rock, a Refuge, undergirds you with the Everlasting Arms.

PRAYER PETITION:

We feel safe, a Father, when we take refuge in Thy everlasting arms. May we let go of self, as we drop back into Thy always outstretched arms.

DECEMBER 10

Judge not, that ye be not judged. -MATT. 7:1.

This is the hardest thing for a Christian to learn. Some of the saintliest souls I know have this sin of Pharisaism. The ability to see

wrong in others is born of the wrong within ourselves. The truism, "evil to him who evil thinks" is not far amiss. God alone can judge. No human judgment is infallible. It were better far, for our own good, if destructive criticism of another were never uttered, or even thought.

PRAYER SUGGESTION:

This text suggests the prayer which we each need to pray. Pray that we may not judge. No one of us is without fault. Why criticize others?

DECEMBER 11

I will surely do thee good. -GEN. 32:12.

The greatest proof of God is that companion-ship with Him never leads to wrong doing. Association with God produces but one thing -the good. Physical- mental and spiritual benefits come through following Him.

PRAYER PETITION:

Thou doest good unto me continually. Thou assurest me that Thou wilt ever continue to do good. Thank Thee, Lord.

DECEMBER 12

And I will put enmity between thee and the woman, and between thy seed and her

seed, -GENESIS 3:15-The first and all-
Comprehensive Prophecy.

From now until Christmas we shall make a
study of events leading to the Birth of Christ.
To begin such a study we must begin with
Messianic Prophecies. This is the first one in
the Bible. It promises the coming of One, the
seed of a woman, who shall bruise the head of
the serpent.

PRAYER PETITION:

We realize how true it is that all through
the ages there is strife between the Son of Man
and the Evil One. a God, grant that we
may trample with firmness upon the head of
Evil.

DECEMBER 13

*Behold, a virgin shall conceive, and bear a
son, and shall call his name Immanuel.* -ISAIAH
7:14.

Isaiah predicted that the Messiah should be
born of a virgin and his name should be Immanuel.
This prophecy was made several hundred
years before the birth of Christ. The
fact that Christ fulfilled so entirely the prophecies
of the Old Testament, is added proof
of His divinity.

PRAYER SUGGESTION:

We are beginning to look forward to Christmas.
Pray that the true spirit and meaning of
the season may become a part of your thoughts.

DECEMBER 14

For unto us a child is born, unto us a son is
given . . . . and his name shall be called Wonderful,
Counsellor, The Mighty God, The Everlasting
Father, The Prince of Peace. Of the
increase of his government and peace there
shall be no end .... -ISAIAH 9:6-7.

Here the prophet makes his prediction in
the present tense, as if it already had occurred.
He herein gives several names: "Wonderful,
Counselor, Mighty God, Everlasting Father,
Prince of Peace." Jesus must have been a
remarkable genius to have suited His life so
perfectly to these prophecies, if, as some maintain,
He constantly bore them in mind and
shaped His life accordingly.

PRAYER PETITION:

For the Wonderful One, we thank Thee.
All that we would find in our King of Kings,
we have in Him. We bow in allegiance before
Him.

DECEMBER 15

Rejoice greatly, 0 daughter of Zion; shout,
o Daughter of Jerusalem ; behold, thy King
cometh unto thee; he is just, and having

salvation; lowly, and riding upon an ass....
-ZECH. 9:9.

Here is described the lowliness of the Messiah.
The prophets were able to depict in minutest
detail the appearance, life and needs of
the Messiah. In this text he is shown "riding
upon an ass, even upon a colt, the foal of an
ass."

PRAYER PETITION:

In this prophecy we find two attributes of
the Jesus' life for which we pray-"he is just,
lowly." Grant to us justice, lowliness.

DECEMBER 16

*And I said unto them, if ye think good, give
me my price; and if not, forbear. So they
weighed for my price thirty pieces of silver. And
the Lord said unto me, Cast it unto the potter:
a goodly price that I was priced at of them ...*
-ZECH. 11: 12-13.

Judas must have worked in cooperation with
Jesus to have carried out the prophecy of the
thirty pieces of silver, if their lives were merely
a hoax. Strange that Judas should have hanged
himself and Jesus been crucified! Their act
played to the end, resulted in bitter tragedy.

PRAYER PETITION:

O the tragedy of selling the priceless Christ

for thirty pieces of silver. And yet how often
we sell Thee for less. All things are so paltry
as compared with Thee, dear Jesus.

DECEMBER 17

My God, why hast Thou forsaken me? ...
All they that see me la1tgh me to scorn...He
trusted on the Lord that he would deliver him
..... My strength is dried up like a potsherd;
and my tongue cleaveth to my jaws; and Thou
hast brought me into the dust of death ....
They part my garments among them, and cast
lots upon my vesture. -PS. 22:1, 7, 8, 15-18.

These verses are prophetic of the Crucifixion.
The first three are not so vivid, but the most
ignorant recalls the last, "They pierced my
hands and my feet"; "They part my garments
among them, and upon my vesture do they cast
lots." Even the Psalmist became a prophet
to help enact the divine drama.

PRAYER PETITION:

Thou didst come to earth, Jesus, not to live
but to die-and for us. We cannot comprehend
such love, but we adore Thee for it.

DECEMBER 18

I have set the Lord always before me;
because he is at my right hand, I shall not be
moved. Therefore my heart is glad, and my
glory rejoiceth; my flesh also shall rest in hope.

For thou wilt not leave my soul in hell; neither
wilt thou suffer thine Holy One to see corruption.
Thou wilt show me the path of life;
in thy presence is fulness of joy; at thy right
hand there are pleasures for evermore. -PS.
16:8-11.

This portion might be somewhat far fetched.
However, to refresh your memories you can
read Acts 2:25-28; 13:35 and Matthew 7:14,
28: 9, and you will see how identical, is the
Psalmist's prophecy with what actually
occurred.

PRAYER PETITION:

We joy in the Resurrection of Thy Holy
One. Without this glorious hope, life would
become unbearable.

DECEMBER 19

No man hath seen God at any time; the only
begotten Son, which is in the bosom of the
Father, he hath declared Him. -JOHN 1:18.

We leave the prophecies and lead up, more
directly, to the Messiah's coming. This we find
narrated in the New Testament. In this verse
John gives us the thought that Jesus had preexisted
in the bosom of the Father. Of course
John did not know that to be a fact other than
as God revealed this truth to him. Neither was
the law of gravitation a fact, until the revelation
of it was made to Newton.

204

PRAYER PETITION:

We thank Thee because we can begin to
comprehend God through the person of Jesus.

DECEMBER 20

MATTHEW 1:1-17.

Reading all these names in Jesus family tree
will be rather tedious. If there are children
in the home and the chapter is read in their
presence, stop at the fifth verse and tell them
the story of Ruth. Such an interesting story
in the genealogy of Jesus will tend to break the
uninteresting list of names. Test your knowledge of scripture and see how many names
there are of which you can tell something.

PRAYER SUGGESTION:

As we read the genealogy of Jesus, we may
well stop to consider what we are handing
down to coming generations. Pray that we
give unto them a strong heritage.

DECEMBER 21

LUKE 1:1-23.

One cannot write of the birth of Jesus without
mentioning His fore-runner. The contents
of this passage should be read with care.
John was born as the result of prayer and given
to the Lord before his birth. Perhaps God

would violate man-established laws of eugenics
if we prayed more earnestly to Him for
children in their pre-natal state.
PRAYER PETITION:

Thy marvelous power is demonstrated in the
birth of each child. We cannot understand,
we can only marvel. a God, may parenthood
be a sacred trust, to be entered and to be
lived with prayer.

DECEMBER 22

LUKE 1 :26-3 8.

Much theological controversy might be entered
into in our thinking regarding the Annunciation.
What more need we know than
what the Scripture says? Of course Mary's
conception was miraculous. Why reason it
away because it isn't the method Nature
employs? God created Nature and if He sought
to do so could He not violate His own
laws? Surely God is not a victim of the .laws
He Himself created!

PRAYER PETITION:

Forbid that we shall ever limit God to the
narrow confines of man's understanding. We
rejoice that in Thy very birth, Thou wert different.
Thou art indeed my God, 0 Christ.

DECEMBER 23

LUKE 1:39-56.

These verses constitute what is termed the
"Magnificat." With such a rich faith as hers
the child naturally took form according to he;
Ideals. The thoughts of a mother inflict themselves upon the bit of life she carries. Aside
from the miraculous element, Mary's child
could not but be a Jesus. Her song indicates
the richness of her faith.

PRAYER SUGGESTION:

Mary's Magnificat finds a grand echo in the
minds of each of us. Read it aloud as a prayer.

DECEMBER 24

LUKE 1:57-80.

The first chapter of Luke is a long one. Much
of great interest is contained in it. The birth
of John carries with it many facts of interest.
He, too, had been set aside for a purpose. Zach-
arias, his father, caused many a marvel when
he wrote, "His name is John." The birth of a
child is not human, it is divine. Nothing in
human experience is so significant as being used
by God to bring a little soul into the world.

PRAYER SUGGESTION:

John must needs have "waxed strong in

spirit" because of the consecration of his parents.
Parents, face your responsibilities with
prayer.

DECEMBER 25

LUKE 2:1-20.

The word that greeted Jesus immediately
His birth was: "No room .... in the
inn." Marvelous that the child should have
been born in a manger. The people expected
the Messiah to be born in a cradle of gold. Nature
smiled at His birth and a star pointed the
way to the manger. Angels praised God.
Shepherds brought gifts; myrrh, possibly foreboding
His death. Words fail. The scripture
alone can adequately give the details.

PRAYER PETITION:

"Thanks be unto God for His unspeakable
gift."

DECEMBER 26

LUKE 2:22-39.

Joseph and Mary, conscious though they
were of Jesus' significance, obeyed all the laws
of their faith. It is interesting that in the
temple, the Holy Spirit revealed Jesus' identity
to Simeon. The deeper things which God
would reveal to us are usually made known in
church. Parents, present your children to God

208

in the Temple. He expects this of you.

PRAYER SUGGESTION:

"When they had performed all things according to the law of the Lord."-Do we even attempt to do according to the law of the Lord? Pray that we may. Then, perhaps the blessing we seek will come.

DECEMBER 27

MATT. 2:1-12.

Even at His cradle, all men came to pay homage. Wise and ignorant, rich and poor, all sought to pay Him tribute. It is significant that the wise men returned "unto their own country another way." I wonder, if they did not return home changed men also, for no one can come into the presence of Jesus and not go home a new way.

PRAYER PETITION:

After having bowed in worship at the manger, forbid that we go back again, Lord, to our former way of indifference. We have seen Thee. May we not lose the inspiration of the moment at the manger.

DECEMBER 28

MATT. 2:13-23.

In spite of the edict of Herod, providential
elements always played about the life of Jesus
God had a Purpose for Him. The protecting
arm of God is ever about the child unreservedly
committed to Him.

PRAYER PETITION:

Thou dost use even dreams to make us know
Thy purpose for us. Help us to be alert always
lest Thou shouldst speak and we not
hear.

DECEMBER 29

LUKE 2:40-52.

There are many significant things about this
narrative. The fact that Jesus grew like other
boys is interesting. He asked questions as
do the boys of today. You will recall that the
parents returned home without Him, "supposing
Him" to be in the company. Too many
of us take Jesus too much for granted. The
parents went back for Jesus. Perhaps you and
I had better go back and find Jesus where we
lost Him!

PRAYER SUGGESTION:

Is Jesus with you daily or have you left Him
in the church, there to remain until you
return to the temple again? If you have, go
back in prayer to where you left Him.

210

DECEMBER 30

MATT. 4: 1-11.

The Temptations are of significance in that
they embrace all the temptations to which mankind
is heir. The three depicted embody all of
which we might conceive. A personal devil
tempts us in the same way he did Jesus. It is
interesting to note that Jesus was victorious
because He was able to quote from the scripture
and so subdue the devil.

PRAYER PETITION:

How we feel the companionship of Jesus as
we read how He, too, was tempted. We are
brought so much closer to Him as we recognize
His humanity. Would that we might
overcome as He overcame!

DECEMBER 31

*Now the God of peace .... make you perfect
in every good work to do His will, working
in you that which is well-pleasing in his
sight through Jesus Christ; to whom be glory
for ever and ever.* -HEB. 13:20-21.

We come to the close of this study together.
I wonder how many have followed the suggestion
made and read one portion daily throughout
the year. If our hearts have been brought
closer to God, then the time spent in preparation
and study has not been in vain. Without
comment upon it may this Benediction in Hebrews

ever keep you in the peace of God.

PRAYER PETITION:

Father, we thank Thee for the year which
we have had together with Thee. We have
been brought more closely together with our
brethren as we have united in prayer. May
bonds that have been so knit, never be severed.
And thine be the glory through Jesus Christ. Amen.

PURPOSE

It is the aim and prayer of the
pastor that, beginning January 1st
in the morning at seven thirty, if
possible, each member of our
church and parish will read in this
booklet the material assigned for
that day and continue to do so
daily throughout the year.

To the women of the First
Presbyterian Church, Pontiac,
Michigan, whose untiring
zeal and devotion to their
church is finding fruition in
a constantly growing parish
this booklet is affectionately
dedicated.

It is believed that Rev. Peterson used this
for his parishioners for the year 1928.

Made in the USA
Charleston, SC
25 September 2011